Manual of
American English Pronunciation

SUPPLEMENTARY MATERIAL

Prator and Robinett
Accent Inventory

Manual of
American
English
Pronunciation
THIRD EDITION

by
Clifford H. Prator, Jr.
University of California, Los Angeles

revised by
Betty Wallace Robinett
University of Minnesota

Holt, Rinehart and Winston
New York   Chicago   San Francisco
Dallas   Montreal   Toronto

Preface to the Third Edition

The third edition of the *Manual of American English Pronunciation* is still the solidly based text which Clifford H. Prator so skillfully put together. A lesson on consonant clusters has been added, and more exercises have been provided for some lessons. An over-differentiated transcription, based on a combination of the Trager-Smith notation and the Fries-Pike modification of the traditional International Phonetic Alphabet, has been introduced. In the main, the format has not been greatly altered. Although most of the changes and additions have been discussed with the author, their inclusion does not necessarily signify his endorsement.

I would like to express appreciation for suggestions made by Professors Peter Ladefoged and Lois McIntosh at the University of California, Los Angeles, and for those made by my own staff at the University of Minnesota.

A revision such as this carries with it both an honor and a responsibility: the honor of being thought capable of tampering with an author's creation, and the responsibility of justifying the faith so bestowed. I trust the new edition of the *Manual* warrants this faith.

University of Minnesota   B.W.R.
May 1971

Acknowledgments

Second Edition

The author is glad to express his deep gratitude to the following persons and organizations who, over a period of eight years, have contributed to the development of this *Manual:*

Dean Franklin P. Rolfe and Miss Margaret L. Wotton of the University of California, Los Angeles, who made available facilities and gave encouragement for undertaking the project.

Mr. Bernard M. Goldman, Mr. Reed Lawton, Mr. Morris V. Jones, Mrs. Merle McCrae, Dr. Donald A. Bird, Dr. John P. Moncur, Dr. Eli Sobel, Dr. Terence H. Wilbur, Dr. Victor A. Oswald, Dr. William E. Bull, Miss Audrey Wright, Miss Harriet Ramras, and Mr. George M. Grasty, the teachers who tried out the materials in their classes and suggested many improvements.

Professor Albert H. Marckwardt of the University of Michigan; Professor William C. Bryant II, Chairman of the American Language Center, Columbia University; and Mr. Harry Freeman, Instructor in English as a Second Language Program, Teachers College, Columbia University; who were willing to help think through many of the problems of the text.

The U.S. Educational Foundation in the Philippines and the Del Amo

Foundation of Los Angeles, which made grants which gave the author leisure to write and rewrite the text.

The entire College Department of Rinehart & Company, Inc., for friendly help and guidance at every stage.

Los Angeles, California   C.H.P., Jr.

INTRODUCTION

To the Teacher

I. What the *Manual* Is

As the international activities and responsibilities of the United States increase, so does the concern of our government and our educators for the teaching of English as a second language. Since World War II the number of students from abroad in American institutions of higher learning has risen from 6,000 to nearly 120,000.[1] Each year more institutions, even the smaller ones, find it advisable to set up special courses in English as a second language. The influx of new citizens under legislation favoring displaced persons has made it necessary for our city school systems to create new Americanization and language classes. In many countries, the U. S. Department of State has opened cultural institutes and libraries to which students flock in great numbers to learn English. Each effort of our government to give technological aid to backward regions means that a new group of foreign technicians must be trained, either in this country or abroad, in a language which will make the exchange of information possible. The Agency for International Development, for instance, is offering

---

[1] *Fact Book on Higher Education* (Washington, D.C.: American Council on Education, 1968).

English classes to increasing numbers of people. Owing to the increased prestige of the United States as a center of scientific, industrial, and even cultural progress, educational institutions throughout much of the world are showing an unaccustomed interest in American English.

Unfortunately, the production of adequate teaching materials for use in this type of instruction has fallen far behind the demand, and materials for teaching pronunciation are no exception to the general rule. Some instructors have been forced to adopt the very fine British texts which were a by-product of the Empire's long career as the world's leading international power, though in no respect do American and British vary so widely as in pronunciation. Others are attempting to use speech-correction manuals prepared for the typical American undergraduate. These, with their literary readings, their emphasis on isolated sounds, their treatment of all sounds and combinations as of equal importance, their preoccupation with clarity of articulation, bear little relationship to the special problems of the foreign student. The latter must learn new speech rhythms and intonation patterns, acquire a more natural and less bookish delivery, form the habit of weakening unstressed vowels, concentrate on unfamiliar sounds, and the like.

The great majority of the classes in English for foreign students taught in the United States are and must continue to be composed of individuals from many different countries with many different first languages. The need in such courses is for materials adapted to the use of students with a wide variety of non-English linguistic backgrounds. Even in our cultural institutes abroad, texts with general applicability will certainly be needed for many years to come. It will be a long, long time before materials at all levels, dealing with all phases of instruction, for all major language groups, can be made available—if indeed we are ever to be so fortunate as to have them.

This *Manual of American English Pronunciation*, it is hoped, will go at least a little way toward filling the need. The text is definitely not for beginners. It is best suited to reasonably adult and literate students who have studied English several years back home or who have had some practical experience with the language in this country— the typical foreign student in an American college or university, the educated new immigrant, or the advanced student in a cultural institute.

It is based on the type of American English which may be heard, with slight variations, from Ohio through the Middle West and on to the Pacific Coast. Living as they do in the region where the process of dialect mixing has gone farthest and where the language has achieved most uniformity, the people who speak this language undeniably constitute the present linguistic center of gravity of the English-speaking world, both because of their numbers and their cultural importance.

An attempt has been made to incorporate in the *Manual* many of the concepts and techniques developed by those who have applied the principles of linguistic science to English teaching. The British phoneticians have not been neglected as a source of ideas. We have also drawn heavily upon the literature and practical classroom experience of our American modern foreign language teachers and speech correctionists. Throughout the text laboratory exercises are included, and suggestions are made as to how the instructor can strengthen his course by the use of various types of recording and playback equipment.

It has been our conviction that, even though these pronunciation materials could not be based on a comparative study of the phonetics of English and one foreign language, they need not for that reason be completely unscientific. We felt that there were large categories of speech difficulties which all or many of our students had in common, and we have found this in fact to be the case. Our first task was to discover as accurately and objectively as we could what these areas of common weakness were. A check list of categories was set up in accordance with the phonetic systems of several languages which have been more or less adequately described by scholars and which were known to us. We included, in so far as we could, all previously noted departures from the norms of the conversational pronunciation of educated native speakers of American English. We then recorded the speech, and analyzed and counted the "errors" of students at the University of California, Los Angeles, for three years. The result was a sort of frequency count of the pronunciation difficulties of a group of several hundred average students from abroad. The *Manual* was built around this count.

Those enrolled in the classes came from all parts of the world, a cross section of our foreign student population. The chief linguistic groups represented were, in order, Spanish, Northern Chinese, Iranian, Arabic, Germanic, French, and Scandinavian. But there have been individuals from all the major language areas of the globe.

We believe we have thus avoided two undesirable extremes: (1) a text organized solely in accordance with the subjective intuition of the author, and (2) one which logically and with equal emphasis treats all the elements of the English sound system without taking into consideration the special needs of the student group.

As the results of the frequency count became available, our next concern was to determine the order in which the various types of speech difficulty found to be prevalent in our mixed classes should be dealt with, and the relative amount of attention which should be devoted to each type. Our aim was to make the students' speech as completely intelligible as possible. Could this be best achieved by treating first and in most detail those difficulties which the count showed to be most common, by an arrangement based on simple numerical frequency? Or were there certain kinds of difficulty which were more serious than others, which affected intelligibility to a greater extent, and which consequently must be given greater emphasis?

We examined with considerable care the widely accepted assumption that "errors" involving the substitution of one phoneme[2] for another—pronouncing *that* as /θæt/ rather than /ðæt/, or *bit* as /biyt/ instead of /bɪt/—are necessarily those which most affect intelligibility, and are consequently those which must always be attacked first. As we gained experience, we were more and more forced to the conclusion that, while this theory might have some validity with reference to beginning students, it was of little value as a guide in our advanced classes. Our count revealed that the substitution of one phoneme for another was relatively infrequent in the speech of our students. Only a few such substitutions—/iy/ for /ɪ/, /ɪ/ for /iy/, /ɔ/ for /ow/, /a/ for /ɔ/, /s/ for /z/, /t/ for /d/, /d/ for /ð/, etc.—accounted for the great majority of cases. Most others, while theoretically possible or even likely, were actually quite uncommon and certainly could not be regarded as a problem of major importance. We found our students having no trouble with /m/ or the diphthongs /ay/, /aw/, and /ɔy/.

We were also impressed by the fact that in almost all cases of phonemic substitution, even in those where the mispronunciation should have resulted in giving the word a different meaning—*bit* as /biyt/ (beat) instead of /bɪt/—, the context made the intended meaning quite clear. In other words, the substitution seldom seemed to result in a misunderstanding. This impression was strengthened by the extreme difficulty we experienced in preparing drills made up of sentences in which either word of a minimal pair—*made, mate; time, dime; save, safe*—would be equally appropriate. Our students appeared simply to fail to understand a word much more often than they mistook it for some other word. We did not understand them a great deal more frequently than we misunderstood them.

On the other hand, certain nonphonemic "errors" proved in practice to be serious barriers to intelligibility, and were shown by our count to be extremely common. An Italian student had great difficulty in making himself understood because of his tendency to pronounce all final stops with a strong "finishing sound." For him and many others, the improper release and aspiration of stops was

---

[2]Sound which may be the sole feature whereby one word is distinguished in meaning from another: for example, *time* /taym/ and *dime* /daym/ are alike except for their initial sounds; therefore /t/ and /d/ are phonemes in English.

obviously a much more important problem than the substitution of, say, /š/ for /ž/.

We found that a knowledge of voicing alone did not enable our students to make a clear distinction between words like *plays* /pleyz/ and *place* /ples/. Better results were obtained when we also pointed out and drilled the so-called secondary differences between /eyz/ and /eys/: vowel length and consonant release. These latter are not usually classified among the phonemic qualities of English sounds.

The author was at one time struck by two very fine examples of how nonphonemic differences in sounds may even cause misunderstanding. With another American professor and several Filipino educational officials he was traveling by car near Manila to visit a school in the village of P̲olo, province of Bulak̲an. The other American asked one of the officials to repeat the name of our destination, and understood the answer to be B̲olo, Bulah̲an. In Tagalog, the native language of this particular Filipino, /p/ and /b/, /k/ and /h/ all exist as separate phonemes. Initial /p/ is unaspirated as well as unvoiced. In English, on the other hand, initial /p/ is strongly aspirated, and initial /b/ is not aspirated though it is voiced. The American, listening to a sentence in which the context gave him no clue, mistook the Filipino's unaspirated /p/ for a /b/. We have traditionally regarded voicing or the lack of it as the feature which distinguishes the phoneme /p/ from the phoneme /b/. But in this case aspiration was certainly the distinctive characteristic. The official had pronounced *Bulakan* with a perfectly normal Tagalog /k/, formed far back in the throat and with a very incomplete closure. In English this /k/ would have been made farther toward the front of the mouth and with a strong closure. Though these latter qualities are not usually thought of as essential to the /k/-phoneme, their absence clearly made the American mistake /k/ for /h/.

When an individual begins the study of a foreign language, the new phonemes are often immediately obvious to him, and he therefore tends to learn them rather quickly. The American who takes up Tagalog cannot fail to become aware of the glottal stop /ʔ/ which distinguishes a word like *batà* /bátaʔ/ (child) from *bata* /báta/ (dressing gown). He will also, of necessity, learn very soon to use the phoneme /ŋ/ at the beginning of a word, as in *ngalan* /ŋálan/ (name), where it does not occur in English. But he may never notice or reproduce certain other features of the new sound system, such as the incomplete closure of /k/ or the lack of aspiration of initial /p/, unless these are pointed out to him. These latter are not obvious, though they may profoundly affect the ability of native speakers to understand the American's Tagalog.

We believe that any pronunciation text which devotes its attention almost exclusively to phonemic differences concentrates on what is most obvious and most easily acquired through simple imitation. It neglects precisely those phases of the phonetics of the language in which imitation is most likely to fail, and analytical knowledge and systematic drill are of greatest value.

Our own solution has been to regard unintelligibility not as the result of phonemic substitution, but as *the cumulative effect of many little departures from the phonetic norms of the language.* A great many of these departures may be phonemic; many others are not. Under certain circumstances, *any* abnormality of speech can contribute to unintelligibility.

This does not, of course, mean that we felt that we could dispense with the phoneme in the preparation of the *Manual.* The system of transcription adopted is almost entirely phonemic.³ We consistently refer to the transcription as phonetic, however, for two reasons: students are more accustomed to this term, and several pedagogical devices employed in the *Manual* are phonetic in character.

We make no attempt to treat such nonphonemic variants of sounds as would be natural in the language of a native speaker of English: e.g., the various regional and personal differences in the way the stressed vowel of *Mary* is pronounced. However, we do devote more attention than is usual to unnatural "foreign-sounding" variants, even though these may be nonphonemic.

The fact that any phonetic abnormality can contribute to unintelligibility does not mean, either, that all departures from the norm should be treated as though they were of equal importance. We have adopted an order of arrangement based primarily on simple numerical frequency, considering first and at greatest length those difficulties most prevalent in our classes. It was necessary at times, of course, to modify this arrangement, in the interests of logic and good pedagogy, by grouping similar problems together. We also considered

---

³The symbols used for transcription in this text are a modification of the systems set forth by George L. Trager and Henry Lee Smith, Jr. in *An Outline of English Structure* (Norman, Oklahoma: Battenberg Press, 1951) and by Charles C. Fries and Kenneth L. Pike in the University of Michigan English Language Institute materials. The symbolization is used solely as a pedagogical device, and although based upon phonemic principles it is not meant to be a "pure" symbolization. Thus the diphthongal vowel symbols /iy/, /ow/, etc. will appear, but not /ɨ/. We have used /ə/ and /ər/ in such words as *alone* /əlówn/, *after* /ǽftər/, *cut* /kət/, and *bird* /bərd/. The /ər/ sound is treated as a variant of /ə/ in the *Manual*, and separate exercises are provided for the two sounds. The "centering" diphthongs /iə/, /ɪə/, /eə/, /ɛə/, /æə/ were included among our symbols as a graphic means of representing the peculiar quality possessed by a front vowel when it stands before /l/ or /r/; we have found the transcription of *will* as /wɪəl/ instead of /wɪl/ a very definite aid in combating the tendency of students to pronounce such words with a pure vowel and with the tongue held unnaturally high. Some means of calling attention in writing to this type of pronunciation seems to be essential.

that an "error" which involved an entire sentence, such as a faulty intonation pattern, was obviously of more importance than one which affected only a single sound.

Problems such as improper voicing, aspiration, and vowel length, which recur in connection with a series of different consonants or vowels, we have treated as a whole rather than as matters to be taken up over and over again in connection with each individual sound. In other words, we felt that the substitution of /k/ for its voiced counterpart /g/ in a word like *big* /bɪg/ reflected not so much an imperfect control of these two sounds as it did a general inability to voice final consonants. We noted that students who substituted /bɪk/ for *big* /bɪg/ also almost invariably substituted /eytš/ for *age* /eydž/ and /ɪs/ for *is* /ɪz/. We consequently did not prepare a separate section and drills on /k/ and /g/, but included these sounds in a lesson on voicing. For the same reason we did not attempt to drill all difficult consonant clusters separately, but treated the problem they represent in a general lesson on consonant clusters and combinations. In a sense, then, our approach has been synthetic rather than analytical.

In its final form the *Manual* has a cyclic arrangement. After an initial lesson which introduces the student to the phonetic symbols, it proceeds at once to the problem of the weakening of unstressed vowels, explaining only enough about vowel classification to make clear the significance of weakening and the identity of the vowel sounds. It then moves on to the closely related and crucially important subject of rhythm and stress in words and sentences. The elements of intonation and the connection between intonation patterns and stress are next treated in two lessons. Until some control of rhythm and intonation has been achieved, drills involving connected discourse may do more harm than good, and it is futile to hope to achieve mastery of the individual sounds which make up the larger patterns. If the pattern is wrong, the sounds cannot be entirely correct. If the pattern is right, correct sounds are much easier to produce.

In Lessons 7 and 8 the principles of consonant classification, voicing, and aspiration are explained and applied, with particular emphasis on the pronunciation of the endings -s and -ed, and the effect of an initial or final position on articulation. Lesson 9 deals with the glides /l/ and /r/ and their influence on preceding vowel sounds, and also with the group of syllabic consonants.

Attention is then shifted back to vowels. Detailed analyses of the formation of the individual sounds are given, and the problem of tonic vowel substitutions is attacked. Lessons 12 and 13 deal with prevalent consonant substitutions which are the effect, not of improper voicing or aspiration, but of a formation of the individual sounds which is faulty in some other respect. Lesson 14 attacks the problems produced by consonant clusters in both initial and final position as well as those produced medially in words and phrases.

The last two lessons of the *Manual* deal with the orthographic representation of English vowels and should be particularly helpful in interpreting the inconsistencies of English spelling as they apply to reading and writing English.

II. Use of the *Manual*

Since the *Manual* is not intended for beginners, but for individuals who have already read a great deal of English and are familiar with the traditional orthography of common words, there seemed to be no advantage in writing all exercises in phonetic symbols in an attempt to guard the students against spelling pronunciations. A great deal of transcribed material with intonation and stress markings has been included, however, especially in the earlier lessons. The purpose of these transcriptions is to facilitate the breaking up of old speech habits by providing a new type of visual stimulus, to make it possible for the student's analytical faculties to intervene more effectively in the formation of sounds and patterns of sound. This effect is best achieved as he first becomes familiar with symbols, and the law of diminishing returns appears to make itself felt soon thereafter. Toward the end of the text special symbols and markings are used more and more sparingly, and the transition is thus made back to normal orthography, to the language situation in which the student has been finding himself all along in his other classes and in which he will continue to use English.

It was never intended that the *Manual* should teach students to make phonetic transcriptions and to mark intonation themselves. All that is aimed at is an ability to read symbols and to follow intonation lines. It is true that in several cases the class is asked to transcribe and mark the intonation patterns of a few carefully chosen sentences. The purpose of these exercises, however, is merely to achieve passive recognition more rapidly by means of a little active experience. The instructor is strongly warned against making the ability to write in phonetic symbols an end in itself.

The instructor should also be warned against teaching the analytical material directly to the students; it is rather to be used indirectly as a means of helping them with the specific problems introduced in each lesson. After the lesson has been presented and practiced in class, students can be directed to pertinent explanatory sections if the instructor feels they will be useful. For this reason, the text should not usually be assigned in advance.

Whenever possible, the exercises provided are made up of entire sentences and even connected paragraphs rather than of individual words. A simple vocabulary chosen from Thorndike's first few hundred words has been used, and the subject matter has been drawn largely from the situations of everyday life most familiar to the students. There are no special review lessons, but every lesson contains review exercises; great care has been taken to ensure the recall of important principles at spaced intervals.

Even so, it is recognized that any course in English pronunciation which asked of its students no more than the completion of the work prescribed in the pages of this *Manual* would be woefully incomplete. Analytical explanations and controlled drills such as those of the text certainly are a necessary part of a pronunciation course; there seems to be no other way to break up deeply ingrained habits of faulty speech and to initiate the formation of new habits. But the best way to learn pronunciation is by pronouncing. There is no substitute for extensive imitation and practice under conditions approaching those of everyday life as nearly as possible. No textbook, no amount of analytical work, can fully supply this need.

It is therefore hoped that the instructor will supplement the work of the text in various ways. He should encourage his students to carry on, outside of class, the oral reading suggested at the end of almost every lesson, and he should make additional suggestions, urging that even more such reading be done. Better integration will be secured if the materials read are those used in other phases of the student's work in English, or in his classes in other subjects. That is why relatively few readings have been included in the *Manual* itself. During reading practice, the student's attention should be focused on one type of difficulty: for example, final -ed, or the stress of compound words. This will give purpose and direction to his reading, and perhaps enable him to progress from the point at which he can avoid a given "error" by conscious effort to the point where he makes the correct sound automatically when he is thinking only of the meaning of his words.

With the same end in view, we have done quite a bit of play-reading in our classes at the University of California. Using such props as the classroom can afford, and with books in hand, the students read the lines and walk through the actions. In selecting plays, we give preference to those which are written in a simple modern conversational language free from dialectal peculiarities. A large cast and well-distributed lines are also advantages, as they make it possible for more individuals to participate. We have found Thornton Wilder's *Our Town* and Hart and Kaufman's *You Can't Take It with You* to be quite suitable. While the play is going on, coaching from the insructor is kept at an absolute minimum, but the attention of the participants is focused on some particular speech problem. Sometimes the text is prepared in advance by marking all words in which the particular problem occurs: for example, all final s's.

The supplementary practice may also take the form of reading by the instructor and direct imitation on the part of the students.

It should be kept in mind, however, that most language is not read, but is in the form of free conversation, for which an exclusive diet of reading is inadequate preparation. In several of the lessons, devices are suggested whereby the instructor can get his students to carry on a more or less spontaneous conversation, while he listens to hear whether they produce certain sounds or patterns correctly. It is hoped that time will be found in the class for many more such exercises. Rising intonation could be practiced by asking members of the group to question one another about their plans for the future. Syllabic consonants could be drilled by writing on the blackboard a list of words containing such sounds, and asking the students to tell if any of these words have interesting associations for them. This kind of work fixes attention on thought content rather than sound production. If skillfully carried out, it can have great value as a means of progressing gradually from the conscious to the unconscious control of a feature of pronunciation, as a way of adding one more analyzed element to the synthesis of normal speech.

How much time would be required for completion of the *Manual* within the framework of a course such as is here described? Ideally, three instructional hours per week for two semesters, a total of approximately ninety hours, would not be excessive. The entire program—text, laboratory work with recording equipment, supplementary reading, and conversational practice—could be effectively developed within a course of those dimensions. Unfortunately, that much time will often not be available, especially if pronunciation is to be taught only as one phase of a general course in English for foreign students.

If forced to eliminate items from the program, the author would probably first omit Lessons 15 and 16, which deal with the relationship between the traditional spelling and the pronunciation of words. Vital as laboratory work is, it is also very time-consuming, and a great deal of it simply cannot be carried out in a short course. The teacher may find throughout the text an occasional long exercise which, in case of necessity, can be omitted. Lessons 1 through 9 constitute, in our opinion, the hard core of the book. With a small, well-prepared group, some practical results might be achieved in as little as thirty hours of class time.

III. Use of the "Accent Inventory"

The "Accent Inventory" of the *Manual* should be of service to resourceful teachers in a wide variety of ways. Here we can only suggest some of the fundamental and particularly effective uses to which it may be put, as shown by actual classroom experience.

As its name suggests, the basic function of the "Inventory" is to make it possible to take stock of the types of difficulty each student is having with English speech at the beginning of the semester's or year's work. It provides a diagnosis of individual weaknesses and a prescription of corrective measures. It should also facilitate the teacher's task of deciding which sections of the *Manual* are to be stressed in work with the entire class.

The "Diagnostic Passage" is recorded in permanent form by each student as early in the course as possible. This passage, on which the "Inventory" is based, is only eleven sentences long. Admittedly, somewhat more revealing results might be achieved if the analysis could be based on a large volume of spontaneous conversational material, rather than on a few sentences to be read. Students do get tense when they know they are being tested, and the intonations of oral reading may often vary from those of ordinary conversation. The conversation-based inventory, however, because of the tremendous amount of time and ingenuity it requires, can hardly be carried out effectively and systematically with an entire class. The reading of these sentences is a practical substitute, which will be valid to the extent that the teacher succeeds in putting each student at his ease when the recording is made, and getting him to read naturally and informally. The sentences should be treated, so far as possible, as a matter-of-fact conversation, involving no unusual emotion or stresses.

Based as it is on the reading of a very small amount of material, the inventory can probably be well carried out only if the "Diagnostic Passage" is recorded. No teacher's ear and hand would be quick enough to note all the elements of faulty diction while listening to a single reading of so brief a passage. And repeated readings always vary slightly. A recording, on the other hand, may be played any number of times as the diagnostician jots down what he hears.

The student is requested to make this initial recording with nothing more in the way of preparation than a casual preliminary reading of the "Diagnostic Passage" at home to familiarize himself with the thought of the sentences. If the teacher will record his own "correct" version of each sentence immediately after the student's version, the subsequent usefulness of the recording will be increased.

The teacher then analyzes each student's version of the eleven sentences. The "Inventory" is printed as a separate booklet so that the copy of each member of the class may be taken up and kept while this process is going on. The teacher plays each recording repeatedly and makes notes of "errors" heard until he feels his analysis is reasonably complete. The various classifications of the "Check List of Errors" should help the inexperienced diagnostician listen systematically and recognize some elements of the foreign "accent" which he or she might not otherwise have noticed. For this analytical work, a playback machine with a foot pedal by means of which the pickup arm can be controlled automatically is extremely useful. With such a pedal, the machine may be stopped and started instantaneously without tone distortion, and may be made to repeat sentences and even words. Tape recorders, however, are probably more easily available in language laboratories and can be used very effectively. For note-taking and as an office record, the teacher may find it convenient to have on hand a supply of mimeographed copies of the "Diagnostic Passage."

When he has made adequate notes, the teacher or a laboratory assistant corrects the "Diagnostic Passage" and marks the appropriate items in the "Check List of Errors" in each student's booklet.

In phrases like *let me* (Sentence 10), if the t̲ is merely pronounced with too much aspiration, the error is classified under Section IV-E of the "Check List"; on the other hand, if the student, in his efforts to pronounce t̲ clearly, goes so far as to insert an /ə/ between t̲ and m̲, in addition to aspirating the t̲, and thus disturbs the rhythm of the sentence, the error is classified under I-D-1. Because of the arrangement of the *Manual* and the fact that errors in the pronunciation of -e̲d̲ and -s̲ may involve vowels as well as consonants, it seemed best to make separate headings in the "Check List" (V-A and B) to cover errors of choice between /d/–/t/–/ɪd/ and /z/–/s/–/ɪz/. If -e̲d̲ or -s̲ is omitted altogether, the error should be noted under IV-H-2-5. In the case of errors involving a front vowel before /l/ or /r/, as in *feel* (Sentence 9), the substitution of /fiyl/ for /fiə̲l/ should be noted under V-D.

The corrected and marked copies of the "Inventory" booklets are not returned to the students until the latter have completed their study of at least the first four or five lessons of the *Manual*, and can therefore be expected to recognize most of the symbols used and understand something of the principles involved. At the time the booklets are returned, every effort should be made to impress on the class the significance of this diagnosis and prescription. It should be pointed out that each heading of the "Check List" contains a reference to the section of the *Manual* in which that particular type of speech difficulty is treated. The booklet will serve as an individual guide to the text. Every member of the class should study his own weaknesses carefully. He should mark in some way those sections of the *Manual* which are of particular concern to him, and which he should review or concentrate his future attention on.

When the student has had time to study his diagnosis, he is given an opportunity individually or in class to listen as his recording is played. The purpose of this is to permit him to "hear his own mistakes," a very necessary first step in accent correction. Clear realization of shortcomings must precede improvement. As he listens to himself, the student should have before his eyes the corrected "Diagnostic Passage" in his booklet.

The class will have many occasions for extensive pronunciation work of various kinds in the sixteen lessons which make up the body of the *Manual*, and in the additional oral reading and conversation which may be suggested by the instructor. The "Inventory," on the other hand, can be used to motivate complementary *intensive* exercise— frequently repeated drills concentrated on a very small amount of material with absolute mastery as the aim in view. If a student could succeed in learning to repeat just the eleven sentences of the "Diagnostic Passage" perfectly, without trace of "accent," it would mean that he had probably acquired sufficient control over his organs of speech to enable him eventually to correct all his faulty speech habits. Perfection in these eleven sentences may therefore be urged on the class as one of the specific objectives of the course.

The drills aimed at the achievement of such mastery may take various forms. The student should certainly repeat the sentences as often as possible. In his laboratory period he may play his recording frequently, and try to imitate the teacher's "correct" version of each sentence. A particularly effective type of intensive drill may be carried out if there is available a playback machine with a foot pedal which controls its pickup arm—the mechanism mentioned in a preceding paragraph. By means of this pedal, the machine can be made to repeat each of the teacher's "correct" sentences many times at quick, regular intervals. The student first listens, then imitates again and again, paying particular attention to timing, intonation, and the grouping of words. When the teacher or laboratory assistant thinks the imitation is rather good, he stops the machine and lets the student repeat the sentence two or three times more in the same rhythm, without the accompaniment of the recorded voice.

New recordings of the "Diagnostic Passage" may, of course, be made at any time during the term. A last recording and quick analysis, carried out as part of the final examination, will help the teacher assign grades based on objective evidence of practical achievement. This chance to hear himself again at the end of the course, and to compare his speech at that time with his earliest efforts, should send the conscientious student away from the class with a most gratifying realization of the progress he has made.

Contents

Preface to the Third Edition   *v*
Acknowledgments (Second Edition)   *vii*

INTRODUCTION: **To the Teacher**   ix

    I. What the *Manual* Is;   II. Use of the *Manual*;   III.
Use of the "Accent Inventory"

LESSON 1   **The Phonetic Alphabet**   1

    I. Learning to Pronounce English;   II. Why a Phonetic
Alphabet?;   III. Table of Symbols;   IV. How Words
Are Transcribed;   V. Exercises

LESSON 2   **Classification of Vowels**   10

    I. The Five Fundamental Vowels;   II. The Eleven
Vowels of American English;   III. Exercises

LESSON 3   **Unstressed Vowels**   17

    I. The Importance of Stress;   II. The Pronunciation of
Unstressed Vowels;   III. Where the Stress Falls;   IV.
Exercises

LESSON 4   **Sentence-Stress and Rhythm**   25

I. Stress in Groups of Words;   II. Which Words Should
Be Stressed?;   III. Pronunciation of Unstressed Words of
One Syllable;   IV. Thought Groups and Blending;   V.
Exercises

LESSON 5   **Rising-Falling Intonation**   41

I. What Intonation Is;   II. Rising-Falling Intonation;
III. Exercises

LESSON 6   **Rising Intonation**   54

I. The Use of Rising Intonation;   II. Nonfinal Intonation;   III. When the High Note Does Not Coincide with
the Last Sentence-Stress;   IV. Other Types of Intonation;
V. Exercises

LESSON 7   **Classification of Consonants; the Endings -s
and -ed**   76

I. Voiced and Voiceless Sounds;   II. Stops and Con-
tinuants, Sibilants;   III. Point of Articulation;   IV.
Pronunciation of -ed;   V. Pronunciation of -s;   VI.
Exercises

LESSON 8   **Initial and Final Consonants**   86

I. The Aspiration of Initial Stop Consonants;   II. The
Lengthening of Vowels before Final Consonants;   III.
Forceful Articulation of Consonants;   IV. Exercises

LESSON 9   **L, R, and Syllabic Consonants**   95

I. The Formation of /l/ and /r/;   II. /l/ and /r/
after Front Vowels;   III. Syllabic Consonants;   IV.
Exercises

LESSON 10   **Front Vowels**   106

I. Vowel Substitutions;   II. The Vowel /iy/ as in *beat*;
III. /ɪ/ as in *bit*;   IV. /ey/ as in *bait*;   V. /ɛ/ as in
bet;   VI. /æ/ as in *bat*;   VII. Exercises

LESSON 11   **Central and Back Vowels**   116

I. The Vowel /a/ as in *pot*;   II. /ɔ/ as in *bought*;
III. /ow/ as in *boat*;   IV. /ʊ/ as in *put*;   V. /uw/
as in *boot*;   VI. /ə/ as in *but*; and /ər/ as in *bird*;   VII.
Exercises

LESSON 12   **Consonant Substitutions: Part 1**   127

I. Consonant Substitutions;   II. /t/ and /θ/, /d/ and
/ð/;   III. /dž/ and /y/;   IV. /š/ and /tš/;   V.
Exercises

LESSON 13   **Consonant Substitutions: Part 2**   137

I. /b/, /v/, /w/, and /hw/;   II. Final /n/, /ŋ/, and
/ŋk/;   III. /h/;   IV. Exercises

LESSON 14   **Consonant Clusters**   149

I. Problems with Consonant Clusters;   II. Consonant
Clusters in Initial Position;   III. Initial s Followed by a
Consonant;   IV. Consonant Clusters in Final Position;
V. Simplification of Consonant Clusters;   VI. Exercises

LESSON 15   **Long and Short Vowels**   159

I. The Theory of Long and Short Vowels;   II. Stressed
Vowels Followed by a Consonant, Then by Another Vowel
Sound;   III. Limitations and Values of the Theory;
IV. Exercises

LESSON 16   **Spelling and Vowel Sounds**   170

I. The Relationship between Spelling and Sound;   II.
The Pronunciation of Stressed Vowels;   III. Exercises

The Phonetic Alphabet

I. Learning to Pronounce English

The fundamental method by which a student learns to pronounce English is by imitating the pronunciation of English-speaking persons. During this course you will have many opportunities to imitate the speech of your instructor and others; do so as accurately and as often as you can. The strange new sounds and rhythms may seem a little funny at first, but you must try to forget that, and imitate without reservations. You have probably been amused at the peculiarities in the speech of an American pronouncing, or attempting to pronounce, your own language; now you must try to reproduce those same peculiarities in English. Your success will depend largely on the sharpness of your ear and your ability as an imitator.

Sometimes imitation does fail, however. The instructor may pronounce a word many times for you, and you still may be unable to say it exactly as he does. This may be because you are hearing and reproducing well only a few of the most important sounds which make up the word. It will be of benefit to you then if the instructor can *write out* the word for you, sound by sound, using symbols which are always pronounced in the same way. One of the most typical features of English is the manner in which its unimportant, unstressed vowels are pronounced. Your attention may not be called to these at all when you *hear* a word spoken, but you can *see* them as clearly as the stressed vowels in a phonetic transcription. The eye is more

1

analytical than the ear. We can see separately all the symbols which make up a written word, but we can hardly hear individually all the sounds which compose it as it is normally spoken.

Most people learn most things better through the eye than through the ear. Even in learning to pronounce, where you must depend primarily on hearing, there is every advantage in being able to have your eye aid your ear. Something learned in two different ways is probably four times as well learned. The ordinary spelling of an English word sometimes has so little relation to its sound that the spelling is nearly useless as a guide to pronunciation.

There will be times when you may wish to write down the pronunciation of a new word, so as to be able to recall it later. Unfortunately, we cannot remember a mere sound clearly for very long; but a phonetic transcription will make recall easier. When no English-speaking person is present to pronounce a word for you, your only recourse may be to try to reconstruct the sound of the word from the symbols in a dictionary. Practice in reading symbols will help you learn to make accurate reconstructions.

There will be times too when, to succeed in making an English sound perfectly, you will need to know exactly what to do with your tongue, lips, and other organs of speech. For instance, in order to make the t-sound in English, the tip of the tongue touches the roof of the mouth somewhat farther back than is the case with many other languages. Merely hearing the t and trying to imitate it, you might never guess this fact.

In other words, though you must rely chiefly on your ear and imitation to acquire a good accent, a knowledge of the number and identity of English sounds, the symbols used to represent them in phonetic writing, the way in which they are produced, and a few of the laws that govern their behavior will be of great advantage to you and will increase your chances of success. This text is designed to give you such information and to aid you in learning to apply it. The text is not a course in English pronunciation, but merely a useful aid in such a course. The science of phonetics may be considered the grammar of pronunciation; a knowledge of phonetics will help you to pronounce no less, and no more, than a knowledge of grammar will teach you to speak and write.

II. Why a Phonetic Alphabet?

The first step in your work with phonetics will be to familiarize yourself with a set of symbols by means of which the important sounds of English—all those which serve to distinguish one word from another word[1]—may be represented. There must be a symbol for every such sound, and no more than one symbol for any given sound.

The system used in this *Manual* is an adaptation of those used by George L. Trager and Henry Lee Smith, Jr. in *An Outline of English Structure* (Norman, Oklahoma: Battenberg Press, 1951) and by Charles C. Fries and Kenneth L. Pike in the University of Michigan English Language Institute materials. This adaptation is better suited to our purpose than such systems of diacritical markings as those employed in some of our well-known dictionaries. Use of the latter may · involve learning some thirty different vowel symbols with each sound represented by several different symbols. This phonemic representation has the added advantage of being quite widely known.

III. Table of Symbols

In the table which follows are included *approximate* French, German, Japanese, and Spanish equivalents for most of the American English sounds. These equivalents are *not scientifically accurate* in most cases, and are given only because they may make it easier at first for you to identify the various sounds.

A written accent marks the stressed vowel of words of more than one syllable: *reason* /ríyzən/. When there are two or more stressed syllables, the most important is marked / ´/, and that with secondary stress / `/: *preposition* /prὲpəzíšən/.

---

[1]Recognition of the difference between *bed* and *bead*, when the words are spoken, depends on ability to distinguish between the vowel sounds in the two words. There must, therefore, be separate symbols to represent these two sounds. The r in the word *water* is pronounced in different ways in various parts of the United States and Great Britain, but variety of pronunciation does not mean variety of meaning. For our purposes, one symbol will suffice to represent the various r sounds. An alphabet based on this principle is properly called a phonemic alphabet, and phonemic symbolization has been used in this text except that deviations have sometimes been made for pedagogical purposes. As mentioned in the Introduction, we consistently refer to the transcription as phonetic because students are more accustomed to this term and because several pedagogical devices employed in the *Manual* are phonetic in character. However, because the approach is phonemic, we have followed the practice of using slant lines (/) to enclose all transcriptions, even those which are obviously phonetic: for example, /:/ for vowel length and /ʰ/ for aspiration.

The Phonetic Alphabet

SYMBOL	ENGLISH EXAMPLES		APPROXIMATE EQUIVALENT IN			
			FRENCH	GERMAN	JAPANESE	SPANISH

Consonants

SYMBOL	ENGLISH EXAMPLES		FRENCH	GERMAN	JAPANESE	SPANISH
1. /b/	boat	/bowt/	bébé	baden	ban	también
2. /d/	dark	/dark/	doigt	dumm	dan	un dedo
3. /f/	far	/far/	fait	Feind	furui	fino
4. /g/	gold	/gowld/	garder	gut	gakkō	golpe
5. /h/	home	/howm/	(none)	haben	hachi	gente
6. /k/	cold	/kowld/	car	kaufen	kin	vaca
	kodak	/kówdæk/				
7. /l/	let	/lɛt/	laisser	lange	(none)	lado
8. /m/	man	/mæn/	même	morgen	uma	mano
9. /n/	next	/nɛkst/	non	nein	nani	nombre
10. /ŋ/	ring	/rɪŋ/	(none)	singen	ginkō	naranja
	sink	/sɪŋk/				
11. /p/	part	/part/	peu	Papier	pera-pera	pelo
12. /r/	rest	/rɛst/	(none)	(none)	(none)	(none)
13. /s/	send	/sɛnd/	sou	Haus	suru	sino
	city	/sítɪ/				
14. /š/	ship	/šɪp/	chez	schön	shuppatsu	(none)
15. /t/	ten	/tɛn/	temps	Tür	to	tener
16. /θ/	think	/θɪŋk/	(none)	(none)	(none)	cita (as pronounced in Madrid)
17. /ð/	that	/ðæt/	(none)	(none)	(none)	dedo
18. /v/	very	/vérɪ/	vain	November	(none)	(none)
19. /w/	went	/wɛnt/	oui	(none)	waru	huevo
20. /y/	you	/yuw/	hier	jung	yuku	hierro
21. /z/	zoo	/zuw/	chose	dieser	zashiki	desde
	rose	/rowz/				
	knows	/nowz/				
22. /ž/	pleasure	/plɛ́žər/	je	(none)	(none)	(none)
	vision	/vížən/				
23. /hw/	when	/hwɛn/	(none)	(none)	(none)	(none)
24. /tš/	children	/tšíldrən/	Tchèque	Putsch	cha	mucho
25. /dž/	jury	/džúrɪ/	djinn	(none)	jama	yo (when pronounced with emphasis)
	edge	/ɛdž/				
	age	/eydž/				

The Phonetic Alphabet

SYMBOL	ENGLISH EXAMPLES		APPROXIMATE EQUIVALENT IN			
			FRENCH	GERMAN	JAPANESE	SPANISH
Simple Vowels						
1. /a/	far	/far/	âme	Vater	ā	malo
	hot	/hat/				
2. /æ/	am	/æm/	mal	(none)	(none)	(none)
3. /ɛ/	get	/gɛt/	lève	Bett	empitsu	el
	bread	/brɛd/				
	said	/sɛd/				
4. /ɪ/	in	/ɪn/	(none)	sitzen	(none)	(none)
	become	/bɪkə́m/				
5. /ɔ/	for	/fɔr/	note	wollen	oru	orden
	all	/ɔl/				
	ought	/ɔt/				
6. /ʊ/	put	/pʊt/	(none)	dunkel	putto	(none)
	could	/kʊd/				
	good	/gʊd/				
7. /ə/[2]	but	/bət/	me	Knabe	(none)	(none)
	bird	/bərd/				
	other	/ə́ðər/				
	ago	/əgów/				
	reason	/rɪ́yzən/				

---

[2]The student who has a good ear will probably note that the vowel of *but* /bət/ is not quite the same as that of *bird* /bərd/, where the /ə/ sound is given a special "coloring" by the /r/ which follows it. Some works on English pronunciation employ as many as four separate symbols to represent variants of the /ə/ sound: [bʌt] in a stressed syllable, [əgóu] in an unstressed syllable, [bɝd] stressed and followed by r, and [fáðɚ] unstressed and followed by r. In order to require the learning of as few symbols as possible and in following the phonemic principle, this *Manual* uses only /ə/ and /ər/ in transcribing these four variants.

The Phonetic Alphabet

SYMBOL	ENGLISH EXAMPLES	APPROXIMATE EQUIVALENT IN			
		FRENCH	GERMAN	JAPANESE	SPANISH

Diphthongs[3]

1. /ey/	late raise	/leyt/ /rayz/	thé	Leben	eigo	peine
2. /iy/	see receive	/siy/ /rɪsiyv/	fini	sieht	ie	sí
3. /ow/	go coat	/gow/ /kowt/	dôme	Boot	hirou	bou
4. /uw/	rule too	/ruwl/ /tuw/	fou	Stube	kū	mula
5. /ay/	I cry	/ay/ /kray/	aïe	mein	ai	hay
6. /aw/	now house	/naw/ /haws/	(none)	Haupt	au	pausa
7. /ɔy/	boy noise	/bɔy/ /nɔyz/	(none)	heute	oi	sois

Diphthongs before /l/ *or* /r/[4]

1. /iə/	feel we're	/fiəl/ /wiər/	vie (as pronounced in the Midi)	(none)	(none)	(none)
2. /ɪə/	hill hear	/hɪəl/ /hɪər/	(none)	(none)	(none)	(none)
3. /eə/	sale	/seəl/	née (as pronounced in the Midi)	(none)	(none)	(none)
4. /ɛə/	well there	/wɛəl/ /ðɛər/	plaie (as pronounced in the Midi)	(none)	(none)	(none)
5. /æə/	shall	/šæəl/	(none)	(none)	(none)	(none)

---

[3]The diphthongization of /ey/, /iy/, /ow/, and /uw/ is not as noticeable as that of /ay/, /aw/, and /ɔy/, but for the sake of simplicity in phonemic description and practicality in teaching they are so symbolized.

[4]We have found that a diphthongal symbolization of the front vowels before /l/ and /r/ is a definite aid in combating the tendency of students to pronounce such sounds with a pure vowel and with the tongue held unnaturally high. We have not used the off-glide /y/ in the transcription of the /iə/ and /eə/ diphthongs because it would give the appearance of two syllables in a word such as *feel:* /fiyəl/.

VARIOUS PHONETIC MARKINGS[5]

1. ? Indicates a glottal stop: *oh, oh* /oˀo/, as in "Oh, oh! Look what I did" (see Lesson 4, Section IV).
2. ʰ Means that the preceding consonant sound is strongly aspirated: *time* /tʰaym/ (see Lesson 8, Section I).
3. : Means that the preceding sound is lengthened: the /iy/ of *bead* /biy:d/ is longer than the /iy/ of beat /biyt/ (see Lesson 8, Section II).
4. ˌ Means that the consonant under which it is placed is pronounced as a syllabic: *didn't* /dɪdn̩t/, *little* /lɪtl̩/ (see Lesson 9, Section III).

IV. How Words Are Transcribed

Note that the phonetic symbols should be printed rather than written cursively, so that they may more easily be read. In order that words spelled out in the traditional manner may not be confused with these transcriptions, the latter should always be printed between slant lines: *fish* is pronounced as /fiš/.

In transcribing a word in phonetic symbols, the guiding principle to be kept in mind is that the transcription must represent *all* the distinctive sounds heard when the word is pronounced, and *only* those sounds. Do not be misled by the traditional spelling. Silent letters—those not heard in the pronunciation of the word—are not transcribed: e.g., the e̲ in *bone* /bown/, and the g̲h̲ in *eight* /eyt/. Doubled consonants usually do not mean that the consonant is pronounced twice, so they are replaced in transcriptions by single consonants: *matter* /mǽtər/. Two words may be spelled differently, as are *sun* and *son*, but pronounced and transcribed alike: /sən/. On the other hand, if a word has two or more different pronunciations when used in different ways, as has *bow*, these must be represented by different transcriptions: /baw/, "to bend one's head"; and /bow/, "instrument used for shooting arrows."

As has been pointed out, the transcription used in this book provides a symbol for each distinctive English sound. A great many of these symbols—/b/, /d/, /f/, /k/, /l/, /m/, /n/, /p/, /r/, /t/, /v/, /w/, and /z/—are exactly like the normal printed letters of the alphabet; as symbols they *always* represent the same sound which they *usually* represent as letters. These are, of course, very easy to

---

[5]These phonetic markings appear as pedagogical devices in certain sections of the *Manual* but are not a part of the overall system of symbolization.

remember. Certain other symbols are also just like normal letters; but the symbol always has the same sound, whereas the corresponding letter is commonly pronounced in more than one way:

/g/   always like the g̲ in *good* /ɡʊd/,
      never like the g̲ in *George* /d̲ž̲ɔrd̲ž̲/;

/s/   always like the s̲ in *said* /s̲ɛd/,
      never like the s̲ in *rise* /rayz̲/;

/h/   always pronounced as in *home* /h̲owm/,
      never silent as in *h̲our* /awr/;

For some other sounds, the traditional letters cannot serve as symbols, and it is necessary to provide new symbols. Since these may be strange to you, to learn them well will require some effort. Most vowel symbols fall in this class. The eleven vowel sounds of English cannot be represented accurately and simply by the five letters normally used in spelling vowels. Lesson 2 will help you to associate the vowel symbols with the sounds they represent. The new consonant symbol /ŋ/ is necessary because the spelling n̲g̲ is confusing. In words spelled with n̲g̲ the g is usually silent, as in *ring* /rɪŋ/; we could not represent *ring* in symbols as /rɪng/ since no phonetic symbol is silent and the /n/ symbol must always have the same sound. In the same way we need /š/, which usually represents the letters s̲h̲, because the s̲h̲ sound cannot be made by simply pronouncing /s/ and then /h/. The symbol /ž/, as in *vision* /vížən/, is a rather rare English sound, spelled with letters which are ordinarily pronounced in quite a different way in other words. The /θ/ and /ð/ symbols are needed because the two distinctive sounds they represent are normally both written in the same way, with the letters t̲h̲: *thigh* /θay/, *thy* /ðay/.

Not all the letters which represent consonants in English spelling are needed as phonetic symbols. Thus the letter c̲ is usually pronounced like an s̲ or a k̲: *city* /sítɪ/, *cool* /kuwl/. Therefore c̲ is not used as a symbol in transcriptions. For similar reasons, the letters j̲, q̲, and x̲ are not used as symbols. To represent j̲ we have /dž/, which is also used in transcribing the "soft" sound of g̲: *just* /džəst/, *age* /eydž/. The combination q̲u̲ is transcribed as /kw/: *quick* /kwɪk/. Usually x̲ is transcribed as /ks/ or /gz/: *fix* /fɪks/, *exact* /ɪgzǽkt/.

V. Exercises

A.   Go through the phonetic alphabet table several times, pronouncing the sound represented by each symbol.

B. Pronounce

1.	m	7.	hw	13.	y	19.	ey	25.	θ	31.	ər
2.	æ	8.	ʊ	14.	a	20.	tš	26.	v	32.	b
3.	ɛ	9.	dž	15.	ž	21.	s	27.	f	33.	w
4.	iy	10.	g	16.	ow	22.	z	28.	ay	34.	t
5.	š	11.	uw	17.	ɔ	23.	uw	29.	aw	35.	n
6.	ɪ	12.	ə	18.	ŋ	24.	ɔy	30.	ð	36.	l

C. Pronounce these combinations of sounds.

1.	pa	6.	tšow	11.	iys	16.	wɔ	21.	ðuw	26.	awdž
2.	hwiy	7.	raw	12.	ʊk	17.	ɛn	22.	θɔy	27.	ɪd
3.	gæ	8.	džæ	13.	šɛ	18.	aym	23.	yow	28.	ɔk
4.	av	9.	ɪŋ	14.	ðey	19.	yə	24.	ərk	29.	θæ
5.	low	10.	əb	15.	fɛ	20.	eyz	25.	hɔ	30.	ʊt

D. Pronounce these very common words, and write them as they are usually spelled in English.

1.	tərn	6.	sɪŋ	11.	tray	16.	huw	21.	mǽtər
2.	sɪks	7.	džəst	12.	kɔz	17.	hwɪtš	22.	réyzɪz
3.	læst	8.	θriy	13.	tap	18.	smɔl	23.	ríyzən
4.	kʊd	9.	tawn	14.	ðɛm	19.	ðow	24.	plɛ́žər
5.	bɔyz	10.	gad	15.	hɪt	20.	yəŋ	25.	mə́nɪ

E. Can you read these phrases?

1.	ɪnðəmɔ́rnɪŋ	6.	ɪnəmínɪt	11.	təðəmúwvɪ
2.	ənɪ́ŋglɪšklæs	7.	wiykənǽsk	12.	ɪnðiyæftərnúwn
3.	wiərglǽd	8.	ætðədrǽgstɔr	13.	frəmðəθíyətər
4.	təðətíytšər	9.	təðəkánsərt	14.	ɪnðəwíntər
5.	hiyzəstúwdənt	10.	wiərhǽpɪ	15.	nɛkstwíyk

Classification of Vowels

I. The Five Fundamental Vowels

The fundamental vowel sounds, those which occur in many languages, are /iy/, /ey/, /a/, /ow/, and /uw/. It is worth noting that in symbolizing these sounds the five vowel letters of the ordinary roman alphabet are used—sometimes alone, as in /a/, or in combination with y̲ and w̲, as in /iy/, /ey/, /ow/, and /uw/. We have used the symbols /y/ and /w/ to represent diphthongization, an upward movement of the tongue in the production of the vowel sound. The /y/ glide indicates that the tongue moves upward toward the front of the mouth; the /w/ glide indicates that the tongue moves upward toward the back of the mouth. This upward movement in the making of these vowel sounds is a characteristic which distinguishes English vowels from the so-called pure vowels of many European languages.

The relationship of these five vowel sounds to one another may be shown by means of a vowel chart (Figure 1).

The vowel pronounced farthest to the front of the mouth is /iy/. Pronounce that sound; then pronounce /ey/. In moving from /iy/ to /ey/, note that there are two important changes in the position of the organs of speech: the jaw is lowered, and the spot where the tongue approaches the roof of the mouth most closely is shifted away from the front teeth toward the throat. If you pronounce /ey/, then /a/, you will feel the same two types of change occur again. From /a/

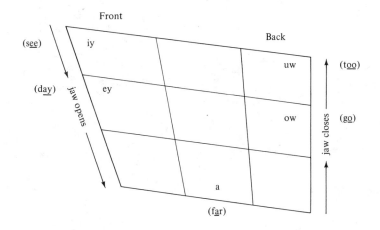

Figure 1. The five fundamental vowels[1]

to /ow/, the movement from front to back continues, but the jaw begins to rise, or close, again; and these two movements also mark the shift from /ow/ to /uw/.

Now pronounce several times the entire series /iy-ey-a-ow-uw/, and try to feel the regular progression in the organs of speech: from front to back as you move from left to right on the chart; and with jaw lower, then higher again, as you move from top to bottom, then back to the top, of the chart. Note also that the lips are widely spread for /iy/, that the amount of spreading decreases with /ey/ and /a/, and that the lips are rounded for /ow/ and /uw/.

Figure 2 may help you to understand how different positions of the tongue correspond to different parts of the vowel chart.[2]

II. The Eleven Vowels of American English

Students of English are usually well acquainted with the five fundamental vowel sounds and find them quite easy to pronounce

---

[1]The vowel charts which appear here have been adapted, with permission of the publisher, from John S. Kenyon, *American Pronunciation*, 10th ed. (Ann Arbor: George Wahr Publishing Company, 1958).

[2]The face diagrams in this text, which are based on x-ray films, have been adapted, with his permission, from those done by Peter Ladefoged. See, for example, Peter Ladefoged, "Some Possibilities in Speech Synthesis," *Language and Speech*, Vol. 7, Part 4 (October-December, 1964), 205–214.

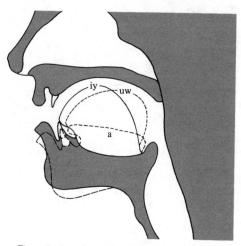

Figure 2. Tongue position for /iy/, /a/, and /uw/

and identify. Familiarity with them may help you to master the six other vowels in the language, those which are represented by symbols unlike those of the ordinary roman alphabet: /ɪ/, /ɛ/, /æ/, /ɔ/, /ʊ/, and /ə/.

The symbol /ɪ/ represents a sound intermediate between /iy/ and /ey/. In other words, /ɪ/ is pronounced farther back than /iy/, but farther forward than /ey/; it is pronounced with the jaw and tongue lower than for /iy/, but higher than for /ey/. This relationship should be obvious to you if you will repeat three or four times the series /iy-ɪ-ey/.

Between /ey/ and /a/ there are two intermediate vowels: first /ɛ/, then, farther back and lower, /æ/.

Between /a/ and /ow/ is /ɔ/, and between /ow/ and /uw/ is /ʊ/.

This leaves only the position of /ə/ (and the variant /ər/; see note on p. 5) to be determined. The vowel /ə/ is the sound an English-speaking person produces when his speech organs are relaxed and in a neutral position. It is the sound he makes when he does not quite know what he is going to say and is looking for the right words: "It's not that. Uh-h-h . . . How shall I say it? Uh-h-h . . ." For reasons that will be explained in the next lesson, /ə/ is also the most frequently heard of all the English vowels; you will need to recognize and make it about as often as all the other vowels except /ɪ/ combined. It is the typical vowel which, more than any other sound, distinguishes English from the other languages of Western Europe.

Since it is neither a front or a back vowel, neither as close as /iy/ nor as open as /a/, it is placed in central position on the vowel chart.

In the combination /ər/, as in *bird* /bərd/, /ə/ begins in the usual position, but then immediately moves toward the back of the mouth as it blends into the complex /r/ sound which follows. Lesson 9 describes the formation of /r/ in detail.

The chart, with each of the eleven vowels of American English in its place, would appear as in Figure 3.

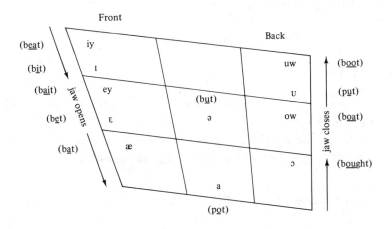

Figure 3. The vowels of American English

When a student of English mispronounces the vowel in a word, what he usually does is to substitute for the correct sound another sound very close to it. In other words, if you mispronounce the /ɪ/ of *bit*, you will probably say *beat* /biyt/. Usually /ɔ/ is confused with either /a/ or /ow/, the sounds which appear on either side of it in the diagram; /æ/ is confused with /ɛ/ and /a/; /ɛ/ with /ey/ and /æ/, etc., etc. Because of the position of the speech organs when it is made, /ə/ may easily be mistaken for any of the other ten vowel sounds.

Notice that a word containing the sound appears in parentheses beside each symbol on the diagram. The only difference between the pronunciation of *boot* and *but* is the difference between /uw/ and /ə/. That is to say, the very meaning of the word depends on the quality of the vowel. If you wish to understand and be understood in English, you must be able to distinguish and make the distinction between the vowel sounds with absolute accuracy.

There are three other sounds in English which cause little or no difficulty for students. These are not included in the vowel chart because they show a greater degree of diphthongization than /iy/, /ey/, /ow/, and /uw/; that is, the movement from the first to the second element of these sounds is more clearly perceptible. These are the sounds /ay/, /aw/, and /ɔy/ which appear in the words *buy*, *bough, boy*. Pronounce the diphthong /ay/. Notice how much the jaw moves. Pronounce /aw/ and /ɔy/. Notice how the jaw moves from an open position to a more closed position during the pronunciation of these diphthongs.

III. Exercises

A.   Pronounce the ten vowel sounds around the edge of the vowel chart (Figure 3) several times in order, beginning first with /iy/, then with /uw/, and note carefully how the speech organs move in regular progression as you pass from one symbol to another.

B.   Learn to draw the vowel chart and to locate the eleven symbols on it.

C.   1.   Phoneticians speak of "front vowels" and "back vowels." What characteristic do all of the back vowels have in common that is different from the front vowels?

     2.   We sometimes call /ɔ/ "open o" and /ow/ "close o." Can you explain why? Which is more open, /ow/ or /a/? /ɛ/ or /æ/?

     3.   Suppose that a fellow student pronounces *it* as /iyt/ instead of /ɪt/. In order to help him produce the correct sound, what would you tell him to do with his jaw, his tongue, and his lips? What would you tell him to do in order to change /guwd/ to /gud/? /gɔt/ to /gat/?

D.   Make a vowel chart and number the symbols on it around the edge of the chart from 1 to 10: /iy/ 1, /ɪ/ 2, /ey/ 3, etc. Number the symbol /ə/ 11. Your teacher will pronounce several different vowel sounds; see if you can identify each by giving the number of the symbol which represents it. If you fail to identify a vowel correctly, note on the diagram the location of the sound you thought you heard with relation to the sound the teacher actually pronounced.

E. Pronounce these very common words, and write them as they are usually spelled in English.

1. læf	9. tšeyndž	17. hwɛər	25. kə́mpənɪ
2. haws	10. ðɪs	18. θɪŋ	26. pʊt
3. yɪər	11. šowz	19. džɔy	27. eyt
4. sɔ	12. wəns	20. lardž	28. θrow
5. rak	13. lɛŋθ	21. kʌ́lər	29. klak
6. seym	14. lʊk	22. ə́rlɪ	30. kəm
7. wiyk	15. lək	23. wɪ́mɪn	31. pliyz
8. ðiyz	16. muwv	24. byúwtɪfʊl	32. ə́ðər

F. Can you read these phrases?

1. hiyəzfɪ́nɪšt	5. ðeykə́məngów	9. šiyəzhə́rdɪt
2. ayəvdə́nɪt	6. hiykənǽnsər	10. wiyšʊdtráyɪt
3. wiykənswɪ́m	7. hárdtəgét	11. ðeyíytənrén
4. íyzɪtəsíy	8. ənə́ftuɪyt	12. íygərtəplíyz

G. 1. Listen while your teacher pronounces the following groups of words. They are all among the five hundred most frequently used in the English language, so you are probably already familiar with their pronunciation. In each group, four words have the same vowel sound, and one has a different vowel. Draw a line under the word which does not belong with the group, and write the symbol which represents the sound the other four have in common.

a. piece, sleep, each, bread, she

b. sit, if, first, him, quick

c. plain, death, they, great, name

d. learn, friend, left, head, next

e. add, back, have, warm, laugh

f. heart, got, stop, dark, law

g. talk, thought, draw, cross, both

h. close, though, lost, road, most

i. book, full, put, food, should

j. wood, blue, two, move, do

k.   does, foot, up, son, run

l.   serve, bird, work, north, burn

G. 2.   Pronounce the groups of words above making a clear distinction between the one word which has a different vowel sound and the other four words.

H.   Divide a sheet of paper into 15 columns, and write one of the following symbols at the top of each column: iy, ɪ, ey, ɛ, æ, a, ɔ, ow, ʊ, uw, ə, ər, ay, aw, ɔy. Classify the following words under the symbol which represents their vowel sound. If necessary, your instructor will pronounce the words for you. Or ask a friend who is a native speaker of English to pronounce them for you.

1.	with	26.	wish	51.	friend	76.	front
2.	ten	27.	say	52.	warm	77.	crowd
3.	strong	28.	so	53.	done	78.	laugh
4.	watch	29.	those	54.	great	79.	God
5.	south	30.	high	55.	bone	80.	boy
6.	late	31.	rain	56.	win	81.	who
7.	bring	32.	month	57.	book	82.	they
8.	good	33.	mean	58.	law	83.	miss
9.	gold	34.	school	59.	act	84.	move
10.	up	35.	best	60.	five	85.	full
11.	box	36.	would	61.	heart	86.	wild
12.	seem	37.	voice	62.	seize	87.	kept
13.	wide	38.	since	63.	mouth	88.	this
14.	off	39.	glad	64.	raise	89.	her
15.	arm	40.	said	65.	cost	90.	car
16.	fall	41.	out	66.	fence	91.	corn
17.	stand	42.	love	67.	some	92.	stop
18.	bridge	43.	put	68.	foot	93.	please
19.	through	44.	point	69.	lip	94.	talk
20.	down	45.	were	70.	soon	95.	cap
21.	light	46.	come	71.	have	96.	church
22.	street	47.	not	72.	touch	97.	most
23.	dead	48.	true	73.	could	98.	girl
24.	work	49.	pass	74.	she	99.	bread
25.	look	50.	war	75.	wing	100.	give

I.   Pronounce each of the columns of words you made in doing Exercise H, in order to be sure that all the words you classified together have the same vowel sound.

Unstressed Vowels

I. The Importance of Stress

We put stress on a syllable when we pronounce it with such force as to give it more importance than the surrounding syllables and to make it stand out among them: for example, the *com–* of *comfortable* /kémfərtəbəl/, or the *–ter–* of *determine* /dɪtə́rmɪn/. Stress is sometimes called accent.

A long word frequently has two stressed syllables, one of which is usually more prominent than the other. An example is *economical*. We say that the most important syllable bears the primary accent, and the next most important bears the secondary accent.[1] In the case of *economical*, the primary accent falls on *-nom-* and the secondary on *e-*. These two syllables would be marked /´/ and /`/ respectively: /ɛ̀kənámɪkəl/.

---

[1]This text acknowledges the four degrees of stress used in the Trager-Smith system but marks them differently for the sake of pedagogical simplicity. The symbol /´/, which designates primary stress in this text, corresponds to the Trager-Smith primary and secondary stresses. In any given sentence, the symbol /´/ is the equivalent of the Trager-Smith primary stress when it coincides with the intonation peak (see Lesson 5, page 44). At other times it is the equivalent of the Trager-Smith secondary stress (see Lesson 5, page 45). The symbol /`/, which marks secondary stress in this text, corresponds to the Trager-Smith tertiary stress. The term "unstressed" is here used to designate syllables which in Trager-Smith terms would be classified as those with weak stress. These are unmarked.

Strong stresses are one of the distinguishing features of the English language; the important syllables in English are more prominent, the unimportant syllables less prominent than in most other languages. Stress then is the key to the pronunciation of an English word, and the location of the accent should always be learned with the word. If you stress the wrong syllable, it may be quite impossible for anyone listening to understand what you are trying to say.

Stress does even more than give character and rhythm to a word; it also determines to some extent the value of all its vowels—whether an *a* is to be pronounced as /ey/ or /ə/, for example.

II. The Pronunciation of Unstressed Vowels

The vowel in a *stressed* syllable may be pronounced as any of the vowels or diphthongs we have listed in the Phonetic Alphabet (see Lesson 1, pages 4–6); for example, /iy/, /ɪ/, /æ/, /ə/, /iə/, etc. The vowel of an *unstressed* syllable almost always has one of two sounds: either /ə/ or, less frequently, /ɪ/. No feature of English phonetics is simpler or more fundamental than this:

UNSTRESSED VOWELS ARE USUALLY PRONOUNCED /ə/ OR /ɪ/.

This principle may be illustrated graphically on the vowel chart (Figure 4).

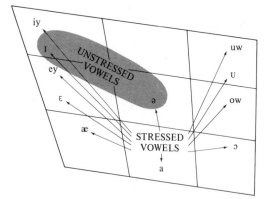

Figure 4. Pronunciation of unstressed vowels

As was noted in Lesson 2, /ə/ is the neutral vowel, the one English speakers produce automatically when their speech organs are relaxed, and, therefore, the one which is easiest for them to make.

An English-speaking person is apparently willing, in a stressed syllable, to make the effort necessary to produce any of the eleven vowel sounds, but he does not feel that an unstressed syllable is important enough to justify rounding the lips, or raising or lowering the jaw. So, however he may spell the vowel sound in an unaccented syllable when he writes it, when he pronounces it he gives it the "lazy" sound of /ə/, or nearby /ɪ/. Since there are more unstressed than stressed syllables in English, /ə/ and /ɪ/ are more frequently heard than all the other vowel sounds combined.

Notice the way in which the unaccented vowels in the following polysyllables—words of more than one syllable—are pronounced:

apparently	/əpǽrəntlɪ/
apportionment	/əpóršənmənt/
congregation	/kàŋgrɪgéyšən/
Episcopalian	/ɪpìskəpéylyən/
insuperable	/ɪnsúwpərəbəl/

If a syllable bears a primary or secondary accent,[2] its vowel may be pronounced in many different ways; but only two different vowels are found in the unstressed syllables above.

Persons who learn English as a second language often make the mistake of pronouncing unstressed vowels the way they are spelled. In your anxiety to make yourself understood, you will probably be tempted to say /æpǽrɛntlɪ/ and /iypìskowpéylyən/. Actually there will be less danger of your being misunderstood, and your English will sound much more natural if you will obscure the unstressed vowels, pronounce them /ə/ or /ɪ/, and make no attempt to identify them as a̠, e̠, or o̠.

Unless you consult a pronouncing dictionary or a competent English-speaking person, there is no sure way of knowing whether the unaccented vowels of an unfamiliar word should be /ə/ or /ɪ/. Frequently it makes no difference; /əpìskəpéylyən/ is just as natural as /ɪpìskəpéylyən/.

III. Where the Stress Falls

Unfortunately, there are no infallible rules for determining which syllable of a word should be stressed. Many times you will need to turn to the dictionary unless you hear the word spoken by someone familiar with it. Certain observations, however, should be of help.

---

[2]Unfortunately, standard English dictionaries do not always mark these secondary accents.

1. The great majority (at least three out of four) of two syllable words are accented on the *first* syllable: *never* /névər/, *breakfast* /brɛ́kfəst/, *Monday* /mə́ndɪ/.

2. Compound expressions:
    a. Compound *nouns* ordinarily have a primary accent on the first component and a secondary accent on the second: *drugstore* /drə́gstɔ̀r/, *thoroughfare* /θə́rəfɛ̀ər/, *weatherman* /wɛ́ðərmæ̀n/.
    b. In compound *verbs* the reverse is true; there is usually a secondary accent on the first component and a primary on the second: *understand* /ə̀ndərstǽnd/, *overlook* /òwvərlúk/, *outrun* /àwtrə́n/.
    c. In the intensive-reflexive pronouns the stronger accent also falls on the *last* syllable: *myself* /màysɛ́lf/, *yourself* /yùrsɛ́lf/.
    d. Numbers ending in -*teen* may receive primary stress on either syllable, but it is best for a student learning English as a second language to put it on the *last* syllable, so as to distinguish clearly between *thirty* /θə́rtɪ/ and *thirteen* /θə̀rtíyn/, *forty* /fɔ́rtɪ/ and *fourteen* /fɔ̀rtíyn/.

3. A large group of words, which may be used either as nouns or verbs, have a difference in stress to indicate the difference in usage. In such cases, the noun has primary accent on the first syllable, the verb on the last (compare 2-a and 2-b above). The nouns in this group of words sometimes have secondary accent on the last syllable: *increase* /ínkrìys/, *overflow* /ówvərflòw/.

NOUN		VERB
/kándəkt/	conduct	/kəndə́kt/
/kánflɪkt/	conflict	/kənflíkt/
/kántɛ̀st/	contest	/kəntɛ́st/
/kántræ̀kt/	contract	/kəntrǽkt/
/kántræ̀st/	contrast	/kəntrǽst/
/kánvərt/	convert	/kənvə́rt/
/dɛ́zərt/	desert	/dɪzə́rt/
/ínklayn/	incline	/ɪnkláyn/
/ínkrìys/	increase	/ɪnkríys/
/ínsərt/	insert	/ɪnsə́rt/
/ínsəlt/	insult	/ɪnsə́lt/
/ówvərflòw/	overflow	/òwvərflów/
/pə́rmɪt/	permit	/pərmít/
/prágrɪs/	progress	/prəgrɛ́s/

/prówtèst/	protest	/prətèst/
/rébəl/	rebel	/rəbél/
/rékərd/	record	/rɪkɔ́rd/
/sə́rvèy/	survey	/sərvéy/
/sə́spèkt/	suspect	/səspékt/

4. In general, when a suffix is added to a word, the new form is stressed on the same syllable as was the basic word: *abandon* /əbǽndən/, *abandonment* /əbǽndənmənt/; *happy* /hǽpɪ/, *happiness* /hǽpɪnɪs/; *reason* /ríyzən/, *reasonable* /ríyzənəbəl/. Words ending in *-tion, -sion, -ic, -ical, -ity,* however, almost always have primary stress *on the syllable preceding the ending.* The addition of one of these suffixes may, therefore, result in a shift of accent: *contribute* /kəntríbyət/, *contribution* /kàntrɪbyúwšən/; *biology* /bàyáləd ̌ʒɪ/, *biological* /bàyəlád ̌ʒɪkəl/, *public* /pə́blɪk/, *publicity* /pəblísɪtɪ/.

IV. Exercises

A. Your instructor will pronounce for you the following polysyllables. First decide which syllable is stressed in each case; then write down the symbols which represent all the vowel sounds in each word, and mark each stressed vowel. Example: the instructor will pronounce *about* as /əbáwt/; the student writes

1. ə—áw

1.	about	8.	even	15.	mother	22.	thousand
2.	after	9.	family	16.	often	23.	together
3.	another	10.	general	17.	receive	24.	visit
4.	between	11.	hundred	18.	remember	25.	without
5.	body	12.	letter	19.	something	26.	correct
6.	children	13.	many	20.	sometime	27.	exit
7.	color	14.	measure	21.	story	28.	mistake

B. Arrange in separate lists the vowels that you heard in stressed syllables and those that you found in unstressed syllables. Are your results in agreement with Section II of this Lesson? Can you explain the apparent violation of the rule found in *sometime?*

C. In order to increase your ability to recognize and place stresses, read this drill after your instructor, and then alone. Watch carefully the pronunciation of unstressed vowels. Note that words with a similar pattern of stresses are grouped together; each group should be repeated rhythmically.

a. 1́-2

1. bury
2. judgment
3. dollar
4. minus
5. nation

b. 1-2́

1. around
2. occur
3. submit
4. disease
5. deceive

c. 1́-2-3

1. vigilance
2. readiness
3. mineral
4. emphasis
5. similar

d. 1-2́-3

1. distinguish
2. abandon
3. eraser
4. delicious
5. paternal

e. 1̀-2-3́

1. overlook
2. evermore
3. premature
4. magazine
5. guarantee

f. 1́-2-3-4

1. memorable
2. personally
3. accuracy
4. amicably
5. delicacy

g. 1-2́-3-4

1. mechanical
2. immediate
3. absurdity
4. catastrophe
5. additional

h. 1̀-2-3́-4

1. corporation
2. education
3. sentimental
4. scientific
5. economic

i. 1-2-3́-4-5

1. mathematical
2. zoological
3. nationality
4. anniversary
5. indeterminate

j. 1-2̀-3-4́-5

1. communication
2. eradication
3. pronunciation
4. deliberation
5. appropriation

D. Pronounce these very common words, and write them as they are usually spelled in english.

1. šıp
2. θæŋk
3. own
4. drap
5. suwn
6. iyst
7. pleys
8. sεz
9. brɔt
10. tšərtš
11. hway
12. gʊd
13. vɔys
14. naw
15. fiəld
16. lərnd
17. krɔst
18. wántıd
19. sέpərət
20. lǽngwıdž
21. néyšən
22. pı́ktšər
23. ənə́f
24. sέvrəl

E. Can you read these phrases?

1. təðəlέft
2. anətrı́p
3. gı́vıtəmíy
4. ıfwiyədnówn
5. mǽnənwáyf
6. fərðəpówstmən
7. ınəkár
8. ætðəkórnər
9. ráytəlέtər
10. ǽskəkwέstšən
11. ınðəkə́ntrı
12. blǽkənblúw

F. Pronounce these families of words, paying particular attention to the location of the stresses and to the vowels in unstressed syllables (see Section III-4 of this Lesson).

1. abominate /əbámmèyt/, abominable, abominableness, abomination

2. contribute /kəntríbyət/, contributor, contribution, contributive

3. abolish /əbálɪš/, abolition, abolishable, abolitionist

4. electric /əlɛ́ktrɪk/, electrical, electricity, electrify

5. apology /əpálədžɪ/, apologetic, apologize

6. attain /ətéyn/, attainable, attainability, attainment

7. material /mətírɪəl/, materialist, materialistic, materialize

8. philosophy /fɪlásəfɪ/, philosopher, philosophical, philosophize

9. method /mɛ́θəd/, methodical, Methodist

10. negotiate /nɪgówšɪ̀eyt/, negotiable, negotiation, negotiator, negotiability

G. Mark the accent on all words of more than one syllable (see Section III-2 and 3 of this lesson), then pronounce the following sentences several times.

1. No one suspected that the runner had made a new record.

2. I don't understand why the class should protest or rebel.

3. They will need a permit to convert the building into a storehouse.

4. They traveled sixty miles in sixteen minutes.

5. The conflict is over, and the coal miners have a new contract.

6. What progress are they making with their survey?

7. The magazine is conducting a contest to increase its circulation.

8. How was his conduct at the concert?

9. So far they have been unable to find any suspects.

10. You will convert no one by insults.

11. You should insert another sentence into the paragraph explaining that word.

12. The overflow from the flood waters damaged the property along the river.

13. The crowd at the lecture overflowed into the hallway.

14. The road inclined slightly down toward the lake.

15. The contrast between the two brothers is remarkable.

16. The desert is a very lonely place.

17. There was an insert in last Sunday's newspaper which was full of travel information.

H. Read aloud several pages of English, concentrating your attention on the pronunciation of the unstressed vowels in words of more than one syllable.

Sentence-Stress and Rhythm

I. Stress in Groups of Words

In Lesson 3, we were concerned with word-stress, the stressing of syllables in words of more than one syllable. Our knowledge of stress must, however, go beyond words if we are to have the complete picture. We do not really talk in words, most of the time, but in sentences, or at least phrases.

In the sentence *I am glad to see you*, there are normally two stresses: on *glad* and *see*. Since these are words of only one syllable, they have no word-stress, but the emphasis that is put on them is in many ways the same as that put on the first syllable of *history* /hístərɪ/. It is sometimes convenient, however, to distinguish between word-stress (hístory) and sentence-stress (I am gláor to sée you).

When sentence-stress falls on a word of more than one syllable, it always falls on the syllable which normally receives word-stress: "I'll méet you *tomórrow*."

In Lesson 3 it was pointed out that there is a great deal more difference between stressed and unstressed syllables in English than in most other languages; this is as true of sentence-stress as of word-stress. To an English-speaking person the rhythm of many other tongues (particularly Japanese, Spanish, Italian, Tagalog) sounds

25

mechanically regular—a series of little bursts of sound all of about the same size and force, like machine-gun fire. English pronounced with such a rhythm would probably not be understood. If asked to draw a picture representing the rhythm of the syllables in Spanish, the speaker of English might produce a line of soldiers of very much the same size and following one another at rather regular intervals, as in Figure 5.

Figure 5. The rhythm of some other languages

His own language he might picture as a series of family groups, each composed of an adult accompanied by several small children of varying sizes. A few of the adults might be childless, and some would be larger than others. (See Figure 6.)

Figure 6. The rhythm of English

In a language like French or Spanish, a line of poetry is usually determined by counting the total number of syllables, stressed and unstressed alike. Lines containing the same number of syllables are felt to be of the same length. In a line of English poetry the number of sentence-stresses is more important than the number of syllables. Here are two lines from Tennyson which are considered to be perfectly matched and of the same length.

> "Bréak, bréak, bréak,
> On thy cóld gray stónes, O Séa!"

The unstressed syllables are so unimportant, rhythmically speaking, that it is not even necessary to count them. When a person recites those lines, it takes him as long to say the first as the second, even though the first contains only three syllables and the second is made up of seven.

This leads to a significant observation regarding English pronunciation:

ACCENTS TEND TO RECUR AT REGULAR INTERVALS.

The more unstressed syllables there are between accents, the more rapidly (and indistinctly) they are pronounced. This is true to a large extent even of prose.

Have your teacher or a native speaker of English pronounce these two sentences for you at normal speed:

> The bóy is ínterested in enlárging his vocábulary.
> Gréat prógress is máde dáily.

Note how he unconsciously crushes together the unstressed syllables of the first sentence in order to get them said in time, and how he lengthens somewhat the stressed syllables of the second so as to compensate for the lack of intervening unstressed syllables. If we were to illustrate these two sentences as suggested above, they might look something like this (Figure 7):

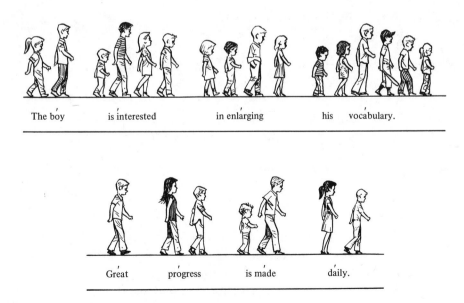

Figure 7. Examples of English sentence rhythm

The problem of acquiring a good English speech rhythm may be divided into five parts:

1. Giving proper emphasis to stressed syllables, and making them recur rather regularly within a thought group.
2. Weakening unstressed words and syllables, and obscuring the vowels in most of them.
3. Organizing words properly into thought groups by means of pauses.
4. Blending the final sound of each word and syllable with the initial sound of the one following within the same thought group.
5. Fitting the entire sentence into a normal intonation pattern.

Intonation patterns will be studied in Lessons 5 and 6, and the rest of this lesson will treat the other four phases of the problem.

II. Which Words Should Be Stressed?

Grammarians sometimes divide all words into two classes: (1) *content words*, which have meaning in themselves, like *mother*, *forget*, and *tomorrow;* and (2) *function words*, which have little or no meaning other than the grammatical idea they express, such as *the*, *of*, and *will.* In general *content words* are *stressed*, but *function words* are left *unstressed*, unless the speaker wishes to call special attention to them.

Content words, usually *stressed*, include

1. Nouns.
2. Verbs (with the few exceptions listed under function words).
3. Adjectives.
4. Adverbs.
5. Demonstratives: *this, that, these, those.*
6. Interrogatives: *who, when, why*, etc.

Function words, usually *unstressed*, include

1. Articles: *a, an, the.*
2. Prepositions: *to, of, in*, etc.
3. Personal pronouns: *I, me, he, him, it*, etc.
4. Possessive adjectives: *my, his, your*, etc.
5. Relative pronouns: *who, that, which*, etc.
6. Common conjunctions: *and, but, that, as, if*, etc.

7. *One* used as a noun-substitute, as in *the réd dréss and the blúe one.*
8. The verbs *be, have, do, will, would, shall, should, can, could, may, might,* and *must.* These are easy to remember, since they are the verbs which may be used as auxiliaries: *He is resígning, Do you sée it?, We must wáit.* Even when they are the principal verb in the sentence, they are usually unstressed: *Hárry is my bést friénd, Bárbara has a lóvely smíle.* On the other hand, they are stressed when they come at the end of a sentence (*I thóught he was smárter than he ís*), and when they are used in tag questions such as *didn't we* and *are they* (*All móvies aren't máde in Hóllywood, áre they?*).

Though all nouns are actually *content* words, the first of two nouns used together ordinarily receives sentence-stress while the second does not: *an apártment house, búsiness affairs* (compare Lesson 3, Section III, 2-a).

Though most verbs are also *content* words, in two-word verbs made up of a verb and adverb it is normally the *adverb* which receives sentence-stress, not the verb: *to split úp, to put ón* (compare Lesson 3, Section III, 2-b). Do not confuse these genuine two-word verbs with other verbs, like *look* and *listen,* which may be followed by a prepositional phrase: *to lóok at him, to lísten to him.* A good way to tell the difference between, for example, *to put on* and *to look at* is to put both expressions into a question beginning with *what: Whát are you putting ón? Whát are you lóoking at?* Note that *at* may be placed before *what* and thus separated from the verb: *At what are you looking?* But the two-word verb cannot be divided in this way: *On what are you putting?* does not make sense.

In the great majority of cases, then, it is a very simple matter to determine where the stresses are placed in a sentence. One has only to apply the principles outlined above.

1. She decláres that she líkes ráts, dóesn't she?
2. I don't imágine you can succéed in a búsiness venture.
3. In an hóur it will be réady to turn óver to you.
4. Thís réd róse is to be plánted hére.
5. He éats thrée fúll méals éach dáy.
6. I shall delíver it to you.

Which are the content words? Which are the function words? Why is there no sentence-stress on *venture* in Sentence 2? Why no stress on *turn* in Sentence 3? Why no stress on *be* in the same sentence? Why is *doesn't* stressed in Sentence 1? Why stress *this* in Sentence 4?

If a native speaker of English violates these principles and distributes his sentence-stresses in some other way, he usually does so for one of two reasons:

1. He may wish to call *special attention* to a word which would normally receive no stress. If the speaker of Sentence 2 above wishes to suggest that *you* cannot succeed in a business venture though perhaps someone else could, he will stress the function word *you* as well as the content words *imagine, succeed,* and *business.* Such special stress on a function word adds a meaning which the sentence would not otherwise have.

2. He may wish, unconsciously, to give the sentence *a more regular rhythm.* In English speech one stressed syllable is usually separated from the next by one, two, or three unstressed syllables. But Sentence 5, if stressed according to the "rules," contains six successive stressed syllables without any intervening unstressed ones. A native speaker of English might feel this to be an unnatural rhythm and instinctively suppress some of the stresses: *He eats thrée full méals each dáy.* Sentence 6, if stressed according to the "rules," ends in a series of four unstressed syllables. The native speaker might therefore find it natural to stress the function word *to* as well as the content word *deliver: I shall delíver it tó you.*

The student of English should not, however, allow these unusual stresses which he may occasionally hear to confuse him and lead him to distribute his stresses carelessly. The basic principles—content words stressed, function words unstressed—are easy to follow. Particular care should be taken to resist the tendency, widespread among those learning English as a foreign language, to stress auxiliary verbs (*can, may,* etc.), peronal pronouns (*I, you, he,* etc.), and possessive adjectives (*my, your, his,* etc.). All of these are *function words.* The main verb is ordinarily more significant than the auxiliary, and *I* and *my* are not as important as we sometimes think.

III. Pronunciation of Unstressed Words of One Syllable

The group of unstressed words of one syllable includes most of the commonest words in the language; the ten words most frequently used all belong in that class: *the, of, and, to, a, in, that, it, is,* and *I.* These ten make up twenty-five percent of all that is written and spoken in English. Or, putting it another way, one out of every four words we use will be *the*, or *of*, or *and*, etc. Unfortunately, several of the ten are precisely the words which learners of English most often mispronounce. *It is probable that in no other way can you improve your English so much and so easily as by learning to pronounce them perfectly.*

The rhythm pattern made up of the alternation of stressed and unstressed syllables is powerfully reinforced in English by the phenomenon known as the weakening or obscuring of vowels. By pronouncing the vowel of an unstressed syllable as /ə/ or /ɪ/, a speaker weakens that syllable and increases the contrast between it and stressed syllables. We have already seen, in Lesson 3, how weakening of vowels works in polysyllables. As might be expected, it occurs also in quite a few words of only one syllable when these latter words do not receive sentence-stress. This leads us to another observation regarding English pronunciation:

THERE IS A STRONG TENDENCY TO WEAKEN THE VOWELS OF
THE MOST COMMON UNSTRESSED WORDS OF ONE SYLLABLE
JUST AS THE UNACCENTED VOWELS OF POLYSYLLABLES
ARE WEAKENED; THAT IS, TO PRONOUNCE THEM /ə/ OR /ɪ/.

Thus, contrary to what is taught in many beginning English classes, the indefinite article *a* is ordinarily /ə/, not /ey/: *in a minute* /ɪn ə mínɪt/. Only in a few rare cases is *a* stressed, and given the sound /ey/: *the article "a"* /ðɪ ártɪkəl éy/.

There are, then, two separate pronunciations of this and other similar words: the weak form and the stressed form. A partial list of such words is given on page 32.

That is weakened when used as a relative pronoun or a conjunction: *the word that you want* /ðə wə́rd ðət yuw wánt/, *I know that he will* /ay nów ðət hiy wíl/. It is stressed and pronounced /ðæt/ as a demonstrative: *the reason for that* /ðə ríyzən fɔr ðǽt/.

The verbs *are, can, had, has, have*, and *was* are usually obscured or weakened, but are given their clear pronunciation whenever they receive sentence-stress: that is, at the end of a sentence or in a tag question (see item 8 under "Function Words," Section II of this lesson).

Whó can /kən/ gó? Jóhn cán /kæn/.
The flágs are /ər/ an éxcellent idéa, áren't /arnt/ they?

Can has the added peculiarity of being pronounced with /æ/, rather than /ə/, in the contraction *can't: I can't tell you* /ay kǽnt tél yuw/. Since the final /t/, as normally pronounced in a combination like *can't tell*, is nearly impossible to hear, a person listening to the sentence would understand it as negative or affirmative depending on whether he heard /æ/ (*can't*) or /ə/ (*can*). The weakening of vowels can indeed affect meaning! If you fail to obscure the a of *can* in *I can tell you*, you may be understood to say precisely the opposite of what you intended.

The vowels of many other unstressed words of one syllable *may* be weakened; the weak forms listed here are those most important to use in order to avoid a "foreign accent."

Words Most Frequently Weakened

WORD	WEAK FORM	EXAMPLE	STRESSED FORM
*a	/ə/	in *a* car /ɪn ə kar/	/ey/
*an	/ən/	get *an* egg /gɛt ən ɛg/	/æn/
*and	/ən/	high *and* low /hay ən low/	/ænd/
are	/ər/	two *are* ready /tuw ər rédɪ/	/ar/
can	/kən/	you *can* come /yuw kən kəm/	/kæn/
had	/əd/	I *had* been /ay əd bɪn/	/hæd/
has	/əz/	it *has* gone /ɪt əz gɔn/	/hæz/
have	/əv/	we *have* seen /wi əv siyn/	/hæv/
*of	/əv/	three *of* us /θriy əv əs/	/av/
*or	/ər/	one *or* two /wən ər tuw/	/ɔr/
that	/ðət/	those *that* went /ðowz ðət wɛnt/	/ðæt/
*the	/ðə/ or /ðɪ/	on *the* right /an ðə rayt/ on *the* edge /an ðɪ ɛdž/	/ðiy/
*to	/tə/ or /tʊ/	five *to* two /fayv tə tuw/ five *to* eight /fayv tʊ eyt/	/tuw/
was	/wəz/	it *was* late /ɪt wəz leyt/	/waz/†

IV. Thought Groups and Blending

By means of pauses we normally divide all but the shortest sentences into two or more parts, or thought groups. A thought group, then, is a portion of a sentence set off from the rest by a pause or pauses. In this *Manual* we shall indicate pauses by a single diagonal line: *There may be time for a swim/if you come at once.*

---

*The words in the list which are marked with an asterisk (*) are almost always weakened: *a, an, and, of, or, the,* and *to.*

†Many speakers of American English pronounce the stressed form of this word /wəz/; thus there may be little perceptible difference between the vowel quality of the stressed form and the weak form.

When we make a pause in a sentence, it is usually for one of three reasons:

1. To make the meaning clear: *When the wind blows/the waves run high.*
2. For emphasis: *Frankly,/I'm disappointed in you.*
3. Or, in a long sentence, simply to enable the speaker to catch his breath.

It is obviously impossible to draw up a neat set of "rules" for the division of sentences into thought groups. Different persons will wish to emphasize different ideas, and individuals vary a great deal in their ability to keep on talking without stopping for breath. A speaker is ordinarily free to group his words in several different ways, according to his personal preference.

This does not mean, however, that a pause may be made anywhere in a sentence. It would certainly be unnatural to pause between *upon* and *the* in *Phrasing depends upon the meaning of what you say.* In general, no pause is made within closely related word groups such as adjectives or articles and the nouns they modify, auxiliary verbs and the accompanying main verbs, prepositions and the nouns dependent on them, adverbs modifying adjectives, pronoun subjects and verbs, etc. But between any of the large grammatical divisions of a sentence pauses may occur.

Analyze carefully the following passage, in which have been marked all the places where a native speaker of English would be at all likely to pause.

> It is not strange/that chlorophyll/has been called/green blood. This substance/is carried about/in little green disks/which,/like the corpuscles of our blood,/can move about/just as if they had/a life of their own. If the sun/is too strong,/they can turn/their edges/toward it,/or sink/to the bottom/of the cells. When there is little sun,/they may rise/to the top of the cells/to make the most/of the light.

Of course, no one speaker would pause so often. If pauses are made too frequently, the effect is unpleasant; if they are made too infrequently, the speaker runs out of breath. If the material is written out, the author's punctuation will be a good guide, though more pauses will often be necessary than there are commas, semicolons, and other such marks.

To distribute his pauses intelligently, it is first of all necessary that a speaker understand the full meaning of what he is saying. And meaning can never be made clear to the hearer unless one groups his words in a clear-cut fashion. The foreign student's most frequent error with regard to pauses is a failure to organize his sentences into thought groups which can be recognized as such. His pauses are too timid, or bear no relation to meaning.

Within thought groups, words and syllables are not pronounced as separate units; they flow along smoothly, without jerkiness, and one seems to blend into the next. A person who did not know any English would find it hard to tell where one word ended and another began. The blending between the two words of *read it* is as close as that between the two syllables of *reading.* Within a thought group a speaker does not completely interrupt, even for a fraction of a second, the outward flow of his breath. The blending is accomplished by this uninterrupted flow of breath, and by the fact that even while one sound is being formed the speech organs are already moving on to the position in which the next is to be formed.

Those who are learning English as a second language often spoil the blending within thought groups by inserting little puffs of air or /ə/ sounds in order to divide combinations of consonants which seem difficult to them: *I don't think so* /ay downtə̱ θɪŋkə̱ sow/. (This phenomenon is treated in some detail in Lesson 8, Sections III and IV.) Blending may also be spoiled by making glottal stops, that is, by cutting off completely the outflow of breath for an instant by closing the glottis (the vocal cords). Glottal stops, indicated by the symbol /ʔ/, are rare in normal English, occurring regularly in only a few special combinations like *oh, oh!* /oʔo/ (to express dismay). In some other languages (Hindu, Arabic, German) they are quite common, and may even serve to distinguish between one word and another (Danish, Tagalog). The student of English should not use glottal stops to separate vowel from vowel or consonant from vowel; for example, the /iy/ and /ow/ of *be over* /biy owvər/ should be blended.

V. Exercises

A. Do you understand the meaning of the following expressions? Each is a phrase of the sort that makes up most of our speech. Each is written as one word, and in actual conversation, with blending well done, would be pronounced as one word. Pronounce the phrases several times, making the contrast between stressed and unstressed syllables very strong. The ten most common English words are all used here, those which make up twenty-five percent of all that is said and written in

English. As a foundation for future progress, can you learn to pronounce these ten words perfectly?

1. əvðəlɛ́sən
2. əvðədéy
3. əvəwɔ́rd
4. mǝbə́s
5. ɪzəfrɛ́nd
6. ɪzəkwɛ́stšən
7. ɪzənǽnsər

8. ɪzðətrúwθ
9. ðətwiynów
10. ðowzðətkéym
11. təbiyhǽpɪ
12. tuəvmɛ́tyuw
13. šiyəztówldmiy
14. hiyəzsíynɪt

15. ayədθót
16. aykənméykɪt
17. ɪtwəzméyd
18. wiərgówɪŋ
19. fáyvərsíks
20. bǽkənfɔ́rθ
21. sɔ́ltənpɛ́pər

B. Pronounce each of the following expressions as a blended unit, just as you did the transcribed phrases of the preceding exercise. Be very careful to weaken and obscure unstressed syllables properly. Sentence-stress is marked in each case.

1. a. supplánt
   b. the plánt
   c. the tónes
   d. the cars
   e. the begínning
   f. that you gó
   g. in the máil
   h. on the róad
   i. with the óthers
   j. for the performánce

2. a. unáble
   b. a náme
   c. a níght
   d. an órange
   e. a stúdy
   f. in a húrry
   g. in a móment
   h. for a náp
   i. for an ápple
   j. at a garáge

3. a. of the wár
   b. of the péace
   c. of his stóry
   d. of a réstaurant
   e. of a proféssor
   f. is of úse
   g. will be of sérvice
   h. is míschievous
   i. the rést of us
   j. the sóund of it

4. a. todáy
   b. to tówn
   c. to trý
   d. to énter
   e. to belóng
   f. to be fóund
   g. to the bóard
   h. to an énd
   i. I cáme to him
   j. he sáid to me

5. a. perfórmed
   b. are fórmed
   c. are bróken
   d. are allówed
   e. are a fámily
   f. we are thánkful
   g. I was ríght
   h. she was afráid
   i. was the spéaker
   j. was a béauty

6. a. submít
   b. had míssed
   c. had léft
   d. has bróught
   e. has devéloped
   f. it has ópened
   g. have becóme
   h. have been decíded
   i. would have líked
   j. may have cáught it

7.　a. consént　　　　　e. can have háppened　　h. I can't sée it
　　b. can sénd　　　　f. he can dánce　　　　i. you can trúst him
　　c. can téll you　　　g. I can sée it　　　　j. you can't trúst him
　　d. can defénd

8.　a. arrést　　　　　e. óne or twó　　　　h. and he díd it
　　b. or the rést　　　f. uncértain　　　　i. bláck and blúe
　　c. or a bús　　　　g. and cértainly　　　j. Jámes and I
　　d. understánd

C.　Unstressed words are sometimes difficult to distinguish in the stream of speech. This exercise is to give you practice in comprehending these unstressed words. Your teacher may want to dictate the sentences to you supplying one of the words in parentheses. Then practice the sentence several times at normal conversational speed with stresses as marked, substituting each of the words in parentheses.

1.　Where did (he, she, they) gó?

2.　Is he (in, on) the bús?

3.　Please gíve (them, him, her) the tíckets.

4.　Do you knów (when, where) he stópped?

5.　Did he ásk (your, her) náme?

6.　You have to decíde (when, where) you're going to stúdy.

7.　When are you going to téll me (a, the) stóry?

8.　What time is it? It's tén (of, to, till) níne.

9.　It's bétter (that, than) you thínk it is.

10.　He gót the bóok (for, from) the librárian.

11.　I néed óne (and, or) twó.

12.　He would dó it (as, if) I ásked.

13.　The mán (could, would) deliver the páckage.

14.　I'd líke thís (and, or) thát.

15.　He ásked me (why, when, where) I was góing.

D.　Here are four series of sentences, with sentence-stresses marked. In each series except the last, sentence *b* contains more syllables than sentence *a*, sentence *c* more than sentence *b*, etc., but the number of stresses is always the same; the addition of the extra syllables does not mean any appreciable lengthening of the time it takes to say the entire sentence (see Section I of this lesson). Tap on a table with your pencil, slowly and regularly, in groups of three beats. Then pronounce each series of sentences several times, making a stressed syllable fall on each beat, and bringing in all unstressed syllables between beats. Each time you read, tap a little faster.

1. a. Dógs éat bónes.
   b. The dógs éat bónes.
   c. The dógs will éat bónes.
   d. The dógs will éat the bónes.
   e. The dógs will have éaten the bónes.

2. a. The cár is hére nów.
   b. The cár is out frónt nów.
   c. The cár will be out frónt sóon.
   d. The cár will be out frónt in a móment.

3. a. Bóys néed móney.
   b. The bóys will néed móney.
   c. The bóys will néed some móney.
   d. The bóys will be néeding some móney.
   e. The bóys will be néeding some of their móney.

4. a. A drúgstore's the pláce to have lúnch.
   b. We shall sóon finish úp for the seméster.
   c. Júne is a níce mónth.
   d. We were enchánted by her intélligent conversátion.
   e. Gréat dáy in the mórning!

E. The passage below, in ordinary conversational style, is to be prepared for rhythmic reading by

   1. Marking all normal sentence-stresses (see Section II of this lesson).

      a. *Forget-Me-Not* (in Sentence 2 in the "Passage for Reading" below) is a compound noun, and the indefinite pronoun *anything* (3 and 5) is like a compound noun; where should they be stressed (Lesson 3, Section III, 2-a)?

      b. Where should the intensive pronoun *themselves* (7) be stressed (Lesson 3, Section III, 2-c)?

      c. *Card game* (6) is an example of two nouns used together; position of stress (Section II of this lesson)?

      d. *Call out* (3 and 6), and *put down* (3 and 6) are two-word verbs; position of stress (Section II of this lesson)? Are *comes to* (3) and *think of* (5) two-word verbs?

      e. Would you stress *because* (7), *you* (8), *is* (8)? Why, or why not?

2. Marking also any special stresses you think should be made (see last two paragraphs of Section II of this lesson.)

    a. Do you see any function words—which, of course, would normally be left unstressed—to which special attention should be called? Sentence 5? Sentence 6?

    b. Do you find any places where it might be well to violate the normal principles of sentence-stress in order to secure a more regular rhythm? Sentence 3?

3. Setting off thought groups by inserting (/) wherever you feel a pause should be made (Section IV of this lesson).

    a. Would you pause after *that* (1), *first* (3), *green* (5)? Why, or why not?

    b. Sentence 1 is almost too long to read without a pause; would it be better to break it after *game* or *play?* Why? Would you break Sentence 7 after *people* or *things?*

PASSAGE FOR READING

1. There's a little game I want us to play that I used to play at school. 2. It's called Forget-Me-Not. 3. I'm going to call out some words—just anything at all—and as I say each word, you're all to put down the first thing that comes to your mind. 4. Is that clear? 5. For instance, if I should say "grass," you might write "it's green," or anything else you think of. 6. Or if I call out "bridge," you might put down "a card game." 7. It's an interesting game because it shows the reactions of people to different things and tells you a lot about the people themselves. 8. You see how simple and easy it is?[1]

Naturally it is not expected or desired that all students should mark this passage alike. After you have marked it, read it several times, making sentence-stresses recur rhythmically and blending the words in each thought group. If the teacher finds that you tend to break up thought groups with glottal stops or otherwise, it may help you prevent this if you will draw a line linking words or syllables between which you are likely to interrupt the flow of breath: say each (3), different things (7).

---

[1]Adapted from *You Can't Take It with You* by Moss Hart and George S. Kaufman, copyright, 1937, by Moss Hart and George S. Kaufman, and reprinted by permission of the publishers, Rinehart & Company, Inc.

F. Mark the stresses in the sentences which appear below, and transcribe each sentence in phonetic symbols. Write each word separately, rather than running words together in phrases as in Exercise A. After you have made your transcription, your instructor will pronounce the exercise, so that you may check your transcription with his pronunciation. Pay particular attention to the obscured and clear sounds of verbs which may be used as auxiliaries, such as *can* and *have*. Finally, practice reading the material from your corrected transcription.

1. What can I give as an answer?
2. I'm afraid it will be hard to get back.
3. He says that he will come if he can.
4. I thought she would be pretty, and she was.
5. She has worked with children since the end of the war, hasn't she?
6. Men have shown no patience with it, but women have.
7. The car had been brought, and was ready to use.
8. If I had seen you sooner, we could have gone together.

G. There follow three stanzas of a well-known poem. Its natural rhythm is so compelling that it may help you learn to make stressed syllables recur regularly and to obscure unstressed syllables. Mark the sentence-stresses, with your instructor's help if necessary; note what types of words are stressed and unstressed, and check your findings with Section II of this lesson. Why do you suppose *give* is left unstressed? Read the poem many times, being particularly careful of the way in which you pronounce such words as *a* and *can;* or, better still, memorize the selection.

GIVE A MAN A HORSE HE CAN RIDE

James Thomson (1834–1882)

> Give a man a horse he can ride,
> Give a man a boat he can sail;
> And his rank and wealth, his strength and health
> On sea nor shore shall fail.
>
> Give a man a pipe he can smoke,
> Give a man a book he can read;
> And his home is bright with a calm delight,
> Though the rooms be poor indeed.
>
> Give a man a girl he can love,
> As I, O my love, love thee;
> And his hand is great with the pulse of Fate,
> At home, on land, on sea.

H. If facilities are available, the class could make a recording of "Give a Man a Horse He Can Ride." Naturally, the selection should first be rehearsed many times, as a choral reading; this careful preparation, motivated by the recording, is the chief value of the exercise. The first two lines of Stanza I, which deal with outdoor life, might be assigned to an individual, a man with an energetic, bass voice; the last two lines to the entire class. In Stanza II, which speaks of indoor activities, the first two lines could be read by another man, with a somewhat lighter and more contemplative way of speaking. If a longer passage is desired for the recording, the three stanzas above might be preceded by another poem of Thomson's, the one which begins, "I looked out into the morning," and which is found on page 1176 of *An Oxford Anthology of English Poetry*.

I. While working on this lesson, each student should read aloud, with attention concentrated on sentence-stress and rhythm, as many passages as possible from other books he is studying.

Rising-Falling Intonation

I. What Intonation Is

Intonation is the tune of what we say. More specifically, it is the combination of musical tones on which we pronounce the syllables that make up our speech. It is closely related to sentence-stress. Often, but by no means always, a syllable with sentence-stress is spoken on a higher musical note than the unstressed syllables. In such cases, intonation is one of the elements of stress, the others being loudness and length.

It is possible to identify on a piano or other musical instrument the note or notes on which any given syllable is pronounced. Good speakers sometimes use as many as twenty-five different notes to give variety and meaning to what they say. Others may use a much smaller range. We could, then, mark the intonation of sentences by writing them on something resembling a musical staff.

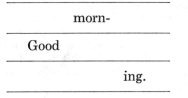

41

Have you ever listened to the tune of your own voice? What tune do you use when you say "What time is it?" and "Good morning"? Can you identify any of the notes on a piano? Which word did you pronounce on the highest note? Which word or syllable on the lowest note? Can you draw a line which will show the tune of *What time is it?* by rising and falling at the proper places?

Each speaker has his own range of notes, and it is not necessary, in order to pronounce English well, for you to imitate someone else's intonation, note for note. What is important is not that a given syllable be pronounced on the note *do* and another on *re*, but the direction of the shift between syllables, the general movement of the voice up or down. Most native speakers of English, pronouncing the same words under similar circumstances, would make their voices rise or fall at approximately the same places.

In marking intonation, we shall use a simplified system[1] which divides the tones into four types: normal, high, extra-high and low. We can then show the movements of the voice up or down by drawing lines at four different levels over or under the passage we are explaining. A line drawn *at the base of the letters* of a word indicates that that word is pronounced on a *normal* tone, a line *above the word* marks a *high* tone, and a line *some distance below the word* marks a *low* tone. A line *some distance above the word* marks an *extra-high* tone, but this tone is seldom used except when some emotional emphasis is required, such as fear or surprise. Can you make your voice follow the lines?

How are you?

I'll have cream and sugar.

---

[1]Much of the material of Lessons 5 and 6, as well as the system for marking intonation, is based on Kenneth L. Pike's *The Intonation of American English* (Ann Arbor: University of Michigan Press, 1946). The chief weakness of this marking system (or with any system) appears to be that, unless it is well explained, it may give students the impression that English intonation is much less flexible than is really the case. One should always keep in mind that, in practice, the voice often does not rise and fall exactly at the place indicated by the markings; the change from one tone to another may be gradual and extend over several syllables. In spite of this weakness, it seems to us that the Pike system of markings is the most teachable yet devised because of its clarity and simplicity.

Usually the movement from one tone to another takes place *between syllables*, and is called a *shift*. A shift is indicated by a *straight vertical line*, as that between *how* and *are* in the first example above, or that between *are* and *you*. Sometimes, however, the voice slides from one tone to another while it is pronouncing a syllable; such movement *within a syllable* is marked by a *line curving up or down*, and is known as a *glide*.

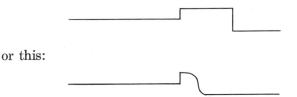

In this last example, we begin to pronounce *long* on a note higher than normal,[2] and then the voice slides down to a note lower than normal before the end of the syllable.

II. Rising-Falling Intonation

Correct intonation is most necessary at the end of a sentence. In this position, the voice most frequently rises above normal, then falls below normal. This means that the rising-falling intonation pattern looks like this:

or this:

The key to such a pattern is the location of the high note: what comes immediately *before* this high note is spoken on a *normal* pitch, and what comes *after* is spoken on a *low* pitch. In a short sentence, if you know where to put the high note, the rest of the pattern falls mechanically into place.

---

[2]Care should be taken to avoid exaggeration of the *high* tone. The examples should not be read this way:

A rise to the *extra-high* note adds emotional emphasis not often used in ordinary speech.

THE HIGH NOTE NORMALLY COINCIDES WITH THE LAST
SENTENCE-STRESS.

Note these examples.

The situátion is intólerable.

I sáid I couldn't héar you.

In both sentences above there are, after the last sentence-stress
and its high note, one or more unstressed syllables left to receive
the low note. The downward movement of the voice is then a *shift*,
shown by a vertical line between the syllable with the high note and
the following syllable. In some cases, on the other hand, the last
sentence-stress and its high note may come on the very last syllable,
leaving no room for the low note which must follow, as in *The cóffee
is hót*. It is then that the voice makes a *glide*, shown by a curved line.
Both the high and the low notes are heard as the last syllable is
pronounced, and the voice slides down from the high to the low note
within the syllable (the phenomenon referred to at the end of Section
I of this lesson).

The cóffee is hót.

Whát tíme did you cáll?

This sliding from one note to another *within* a single stressed
syllable means that the vowel of the syllable will be held for a comparatively long time, so long that it may break into two slightly
different vowels—a diphthong. If we were trying to represent the
sounds as closely as possible, the above examples might be transcribed
as

ðə kɔ́fɪ ɪz háət   (rather than /hat/)

hwát táym dɪd yuw kɔ́əl   (rather than /kɔl/)

These two-toned syllables and the resultant diphthongization constitute one of the important differences between English and many
other languages. Here intonation and pronunciation meet. The

proper use of glides will make it much easier to give normal diph-thongal quality to the right vowels.

The fact that the high note usually coincides with the last sentence-stress in speaking, enables us to distinguish between such grammatically different sequences as the following:

1. Noun compounds and nouns modified by adjectives

    bláckbird   I saw a bláckbird.
    (a certain species of bird)

    bláck bírd   I saw a bláck bírd.
    (any bird black in color)

2. Noun compounds and nouns modified by other nouns

    stéak knife   I'd like a stéak knife.

    stéak dínner   I'd like a stéak dínner.

3. Noun compounds and verbs followed by objects

    chécking accounts   They're chécking accounts.

    chécking accóunts   They're chécking accóunts.

4. Two-word verbs and verbs followed by prepositions

    look úp   What are you looking úp?

    lóok at   What are you lóoking at?

IN ENGLISH, RISING-FALLING INTONATION IS NORMALLY USED AT THE END OF

1. SIMPLE STATEMENTS OF FACT (DECLARATIVE SENTENCES)

<u>This is my</u> wife.

<u>He hasn't said a</u> word.

2. COMMANDS

<u>Come to</u> see me.

3. QUESTIONS WHICH BEGIN WITH AN INTERROGATIVE WORD, such as *what, who, which, why, when, where, how,* etc. Hereafter these will be referred to as *wh-questions.*[3]

<u>What is the</u> matter?

<u>How are you</u> feeling?

<u>Why is he</u> angry?

Persons whose native language is not English may have considerable difficulty at first in pronouncing questions of the type just described with the proper rising-falling intonation. The tendency to use a rising intonation in such cases must be strongly resisted.

---

[3]Some grammarians call these "special questions," and distinguish them from "general questions," which do not begin with an interrogative word. General questions (such as *Are you coming?*) may be answered by *yes* or *no;* thus they are often called "yes-no questions." Special questions (such as *What time is it?*) require more specific information as an answer.

The fall of your voice to a low tone at the end of a sentence is a sort of vocal punctuation mark, a vocal period, indicating that the thought is completed. A listener feels that there is more to be added until he hears your voice drop. A disagreeable and puzzling impression of inconclusiveness is given the listener when a speaker's voice falls only a little or not at all at the end of a statement, command, or question beginning with an interrogative word. Clear rising-falling intonation establishes a mood of certainty and completeness.

III. Exercises

A. 1. Listen carefully as your instructor pronounces some of the material below. Can you hear the high and low notes in his voice? Then, in order to fix the rising-falling intonation pattern in your mind, ear, and speech habits, repeat these short sentences yourself until they sound perfectly natural to you. Make your voice follow the intonation line, and do not forget to weaken unstressed vowels and to blend words together.

a. I'd like an apple.

b. I'd like a soda.

c. I'd like a hot dog.

d. I'd like a sandwich

e. I'd like some coffee.

f. I'd like a wrist watch.

g. I'd like to hear it.

h. I'd like to forget them.

i. I'd like to come over.

j. I'd like to answer him.

k. I'd like a balcony seat.

l. I'd like an "A."

m. I'd like to leave.

n. I'd like a cigarette.

o. I'd like to finish up.

p. I'd like a bowl of soup.

q. I'd like to be there.   v. I'd like to see.

r. I'd like to believe it.   w. I'd like to know.

s. I'd like a newspaper.   x. I'd like to find out.

t. I'd like to speak to you.   y. I'd like a new car.

u. I'd like a ring.   z. I'd like a piece of cake.

2. Your instructor will ask you or one of the other students the question *What would you like?* Answer by using one of the sentences above. You, in turn, ask someone else this same question, and he also will answer from the sentences above. Continue the exercise until everyone has had an opportunity to ask the question and have it answered from the sentences above.

B. 1. Repeat these *wh-questions* after your instructor. Be sure to use the rising-falling intonation.

a. What did you bring?   f. What did you think up?

b. What did you want?   g. What did you think of?

c. What did you forget?   h. What did you tell her?

d. What did you find?   i. What is he carrying?

e. What did you ask?   j. What is he waiting for?

k. What is he talking about?   s. What is he giving you?

l. How are you feeling?   t. What is he studying it for?

m. Which is the library?   u. How did you come?

n. When do we eat?   v. Who wrote it?

o. When can I study?   w. Why did you take it?

p. Where's the Art Building?   x. Which ones are the best?

q. What did you run over?   y. Whom did you see?

r. What did you speak about?   z. How did he do it?

2. Your instructor will ask you a question from the list above. You will answer the question and then ask another student one of the questions from the list. The drill will continue until every student has participated. (Caution to the teacher: Do not allow students to take a long time to answer the questions. Keep the exercise moving rapidly by being willing to supply a cue for the answer when a student hesitates.)

C. First, read over the following exercise silently to make sure you understand the meaning of each sentence. Then pronounce the entire series several times, concentrating on rhythm and intonation.

1. ðɪs ɪz nuw yɔrk   3. hwɛərz ðə howtɛl

2. ay niyd ə ruwm   4. ɪts nɪər ðə laybrɛrɪ

5. wiəl téyk ə tǽksɪ

6. ráyt yur néym hɛ́ər

7. rɪ́ŋ fɔr ðə bɔ́y

8. húw brɔ́t ðə bǽgz

9. gív ɪm ə típ

10. húwz æt ðə dɔ́r

11. tɛ́l ɪm tə kəm ín

12. aym rɛ́dɪ tə gów

13. aym həŋ́grɪ

14. hwɛ́ərz ðe dáynɪŋ ruwm

15. wiəl íyt ðɛ́ər

16. haw mə́tš dɪd ɪt kɔ́st

17. ɪts bín ə gúd tríp

18. péy fɔr ɪt náw

19. ðǽt wɪəl biy fáyn

20. wiəl biy síyɪŋ yuw

D. Be very careful in placing the high note as you pronounce the following pairs of sentences.

1. a. In Pasadena, there's a playhouse.
    b. Most children like to play house.

2. a. I know nothing about that and care less.
    b. He's always a little careless.

3. a. Try to keep the street cleaner.
    b. Try to keep the street-cleaner.

4. a. In India, the British no longer have a strong hold.
    b. Gibraltar is a stronghold.

5. a. That boy has found a bird's-nest.
    b. I've never seen those birds nest.

E. Outside of class your instructor will mark the intonation patterns of the passage below and record the material, following his own markings. He will then play the recording several times, sentence by sentence, for the class. Listen to his intonation and try to mark the passage so as to show what his patterns were. He will probably use some patterns with which you are not yet familiar, but don't try to analyze these. The exercise is intended merely to help you develop your ability to hear intonation.

PASSAGE TO BE MARKED

1. I usually get up early.   2. It takes me about half an hour to brush my teeth, shave, and get ready to leave the house.   3. On Tuesdays and Thursdays I sometimes take a swim before breakfast.   4. Do you like to swim?   5. There's nothing else like it to start the day off right.

6. What else would give you such an appetite?

F. The material below is to be prepared for reading and then is to be read.

1. There are fifteen sentences of various kinds in the exercise. Do you recall the types of sentence in which rising-falling intonation is normally used? All but three of these sentences would normally be pronounced with rising-falling intonation. Try to find the three exceptions, and eliminate them.

2. Mark the sentence-stresses of the twelve sentences which remain.

    a. *Coffee machine* (in Sentence 5) and *napkin holder* (9) are cases of two nouns used together. Position of stress?
    b. Are *cleaned up* (4), *pick out* (8), and *look at* (1) two-word verbs? Position of stress?
    c. Where would it be best to stress *fifteen* (13)?
    b. Would *can* be stressed (10)? *Have* (12)?

3. Mark the intonation of each sentence. First, put the high note in its proper place; then fill in the rest of the rising-falling pattern. Everything which precedes the high note may be marked as normal. Which sentences end in glides? How do you recognize them?

SENTENCES TO BE MARKED

1. Let's look at the people.

2. What shall we order?

3. Where is the waiter?

4. He hasn't cleaned up the table.

5. He's there by the coffee machine.

6. Do you know what you want?

7. May I see the menu?

8. What shall I pick out?

9. Pass me the napkin holder.

10. We'd better order as soon as we can.

11. Will you have an appetizer?

12. We have time enough to finish.

13. We have fifteen minutes.

14. I'll take the regular dinner.

15. Bring us our coffee later.

G. Transcribe in phonetic symbols Sentences 1, 3, 6, 9, 10, 13, and 15 of the preceding exercise. After you have made your transcription, your instructor will read the sentences and perhaps transcribe the exercise in class, so that you can check your work. Practice reading your corrected version.

H. Outside of class, do as much reading aloud as you can, concentrating your attention on weakening the vowels in unstressed words of one syllable.

Rising Intonation

I. The Use of Rising Intonation

At the end of a sentence, two types of intonation are most common: rising-falling and rising. In the preceding lesson we studied rising-falling intonation and learned that it is used for statements, commands, and *wh*-questions. In the present lesson we shall deal with rising intonation, the second common end-of-sentence type.

IN ENGLISH, RISING INTONATION IS NORMALLY USED AT THE END OF QUESTIONS WHICH DO NOT BEGIN WITH AN INTER-ROGATIVE WORD (that is to say, questions which may be answered merely by *yes* or *no*).

Are you│réady?   Will you│réad it for me?

These yes-no questions are easy to identify grammatically because they begin with words such as the following:

1. *will, would, shall, should, can, could, may, might,* and *must*

Shall I ánswer the│télephone?

Can you│hélp me?

2. *have, has, had*

Has he|wrítten to you?

Have they|fínished?

3. *am, is, are, was, were*

Is he|hére?

Were they|stúdying?

4. *do, does, did*

Does he|líke it?

Did they|sée it?

The voice normally goes up to a high note *on the last sentence-stress*, just as in the rising-falling pattern. The difference between the two lies in the fact that, in the rising intonation, the syllables which follow the rise are pronounced on the high note too.[1]

Does he expéct to táke a|díctionary with him?

When we leave the voice high at the end of a sentence, we arouse in the listener a feeling of incompleteness, in contrast to the sense of completeness aroused by a lowered voice. Rising intonation suggests that something further must be said, either by the speaker or by the hearer.

---

[1]A slightly higher note may be heard after the initial rise: Are you|réady? This is sometimes referred to as a "double rise." This second rise, however, is not significant in the English intonation system.

Any statement may be made into a yes-no question by the use of rising intonation alone, without changing the words themselves in any way.

It's time for the class to end.   (statement)

It's time for the class to end?   (question)

II. Nonfinal Intonation

What has been said up to this point applies to the raising or lowering of the voice *at the end of a sentence,* where correct intonation is most necessary and easiest to predict. There is less that is definite to be said about the intonation of that part of the sentence which precedes the last important word. *Nonfinal intonation* may vary widely from speaker to speaker, with little corresponding variation in meaning.

Nevertheless, the student should know that in any sentence we may pronounce on a note higher than normal the stressed syllable of any word or words to which we want to call the special attention of the listener. These may be specially stressed function words (see Lesson 4, end of Section II, paragraph beginning "If a native speaker of English . . .") or content words.

What do you know about politics?   (Note *you.*)

There are lots of cigarettes in the box.   (Note *lots.*)

He has an unusual number of friends.   (Note *unusual.*)

With particular frequency special attention is thus called to *demonstrative* and *interrogative* words.

I think that is a good idea.

What do you want with a car?

In *contrasts* and *comparisons*, special attention is called to *both* ideas being compared or contrasted, but the two stressed elements are usually uttered on different levels. One stressed element will be on a slightly higher note than the other; it seems to make no difference which one is higher. If both ideas are included in a single thought group, the first one will be given a nonfinal note. Either sentence in each of the following pairs is acceptable:

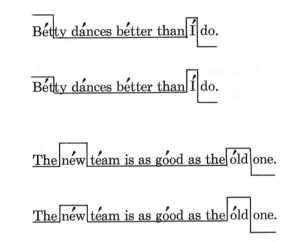

If a sentence is divided by pauses into *two or more thought groups,* each thought group has its own separate intonation pattern. When the speaker comes to the end of the first thought group, he may do one of three things:

1. *End the group with the rising-falling pattern—up to a high note on the final stress, then down to a low note.* This is done before a long pause such as might be marked by a colon (:) or semicolon (;).

I'll téll you the truth:/it can't be dóne.

I don't wánt to gó;/it's dángerous.

Í sáy he cán;/hé sáys he cán't.

2. *End the group by a high note on its final stress, then a return to normal.* This is done when the speaker wishes to suggest that what follows is connected with what he has just said.

You sáy it's éasy,/but you won't trý it.

If you wánt me to,/I'll cáll her.

3. *End the group with the rising pattern.* This occurs, in general, whenever the speaker wishes to create suspense.

When I come báck,/I'll gíve you a présent.

If you wánt to léarn chémistry,/you've gót to wórk.

It should be clearly understood that the choice between these three nonfinal patterns usually depends more on *the attitude of the speaker* than on the grammatical structure and meaning of the sentence. It is usually impossible to say that, before a nonfinal pause, one type of intonation is "right" and all others "wrong." As far as grammar and logic are concerned, the last example above might just as well be

If you wánt to léarn chémistry,/you've gót to wórk.

On the other hand, there are some *special constructions* of whose intonation we can normally be certain.

1. ALTERNATIVES WITH *or. Rising intonation is used for all except the final alternative; the latter is given the rising-falling pattern.* The speaker thus emphasizes the contrast between the various possible choices. In these alternative statements, as with comparisons and contrasts, one of the elements being stressed is usually pronounced on a slightly higher

note than the others. It does not seem to matter which is uttered on the higher note; each of the sentences below is acceptable.

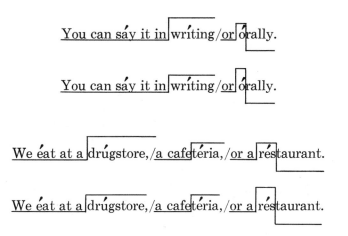

This special pattern is used even if the alternatives are in a question which does not begin with an interrogative word, that is, a type of sentence at the end of which rising intonation would normally be expected (see Section I of this lesson). Notice, however, that the answer to this question cannot be a simple *yes* or *no*.[2] Again, one alternative is usually on a higher note than the other:

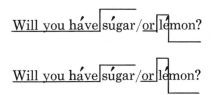

---

[2]This kind of alternative question is different from the yes-no question which may also contain alternatives, but these alternatives are contrasted with one that is implied and not expressed. In these questions the regular rising intonation is used.

Will you háve súgar or lémon?

Would you líke cóffee or téa?

In these questions the speaker is asking if you would like one of the alternatives mentioned or something else which is not expressly mentioned. The answer to these questions can be *yes* or *no*.

Do you drive a Ford, /a Plymouth, /or a Chevrolet?

Do you drive a Ford, /a Plymouth, /or a Chevrolet?

2. SERIES WITH *and*. *The same pattern as for alternatives: rising intona-*
tion on all members of the series except the last; rising-falling intonation
on the last member. As with the alternatives with *or*, one of the stressed
elements in a series with *and* is usually uttered on a higher note. The
order of their occurrence does not seem to make any difference. Only
one order of the alternation of notes is given in the sentences below, but
others are acceptable.

I went to the bank /and the post office.

He speaks English, /Italian, /and French.

3. DIRECT ADDRESS. *Rising intonation is used for names (or words*
substituted for names) and titles addressed directly to the person to whom
one is speaking. These may come at the end of the sentence or elsewhere,
and do not affect the intonation of the rest of the sentence.[3]

My friend, /I'm glad to see you.

How are you feeling, /Mister Roberts?

---

[3]Often the rising intonation in direct address starts lower and does not go as
high as the rising intonation in the rest of the sentence.

My friend, /I'm glad to see you.

How are you feeling, /Mister Roberts?

4.　TAG QUESTIONS, SUCH AS *aren't you, will he.* These show clearly the essential difference between rising-falling and rising intonation. If the tag question is pronounced with the *rising-falling* pattern,

You're hún gry, / áren't you?

the whole sentence is to be interpreted as a *statement of fact,* and indicates that the speaker is confident that the hearer will agree with him. When the tag is pronounced with the *rising* pattern,

You're hún gry, / áren't you?

the sentence is a *genuine question,* which means that the speaker is not sure whether or not the hearer is hungry, and that the latter is asked to confirm or deny the idea, to answer *yes* or *no.* Note that the intonation of the part of the sentence which precedes the tag is not affected by the addition of the latter; though, in the examples above, *you're hungry* is nonfinal, it has the same intonation that it would be given if it came at the end of the sentence.

Tag questions are introduced by the same kinds of words which are used in yes-no questions (see Section I of this lesson).

1.　*will, would, shall, should, can, could, may, might,* and *must*

I can gó, / cán't I?

He won't hélp me, / wíll he?

2.　*have, has, had*

He hasn't fín ished, / hás he?

He had éa ten, / hád n't he?

3. *am, is, are, was, were*

He isn't here, / is he?

I was right, wasn't I?

4. *do, does, did*

They don't agree, / do they?

He finally arrived, / didn't he?

III. When the High Note Does Not Coincide with the Last Sentence-Stress

One of the examples in the preceding section,

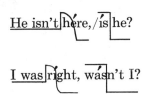

You're hungry, / aren't you?

shows us for the first time a case in which the high note does not coincide with the last sentence-stress (see the "rule" in Lesson 5, at the beginning of Section II). This is because the tag question is very short—only two syllables. While saying those two words, the voice must rise; in order that the upward movement may be as clear as possible, the first syllable is needed for the lower note, and the second syllable for the high one.

A number of syllables insufficient to permit developing the pattern normally is, then, one of the reasons for giving the high note to a syllable other than that which receives the last sentence-stress. This phenomenon may be observed in the other special constructions listed in the preceding section:

Shall we paint it red, / purple, / or green?   (Alternatives; note *purple*.)

I'll have spinach,/carrots,/and potatoes.　　　(Series; note *carrots*.)

Come here,/William,/I want to speak to you.

(Direct address; note *William*.)

If, in one of these constructions, there is only one syllable on which to make the rising intonation heard, then the voice must move upward *within that syllable*, thus making a sort of upward inflection.

Is your name Tóm,/Dick/, or Harry?　　　(Note *Dick*.)

What are you looking for,/son?　　　(Note *son*.)

A second reason for giving the final high note to a syllable other than that which receives the last sentence-stress may be *a desire to single out one word or idea for special attention*. We have already seen how special attention can cause the stressing of a normally unstressed function word (Lesson 4, end of Section II), and the use of a nonfinal high note (Section II of this lesson). Sometimes the logic of the situation demands that *one* word or idea be made more important than any other in the sentence or thought group. The question, "Will you drive to the office tomorrow?", is vague without special intonation. Just what is the speaker asking about? Does he mean, "Will *you* drive, rather than the *chauffeur?*" Does he mean, "Will you *drive*, rather than *walk?*" Does he mean, "Will you drive *to the office*, rather than *anywhere else?*" Or does he mean, "Will you drive *tomorrow*, rather than *some other time?*" In order to make his meaning clear, he needs a way to focus the question around *one* of the several ideas it contains.

Special attention can be focused on one of the words in a thought group by using only one high note, and by making the voice rise on the stressed syllable of the word the speaker wishes to single out, regardless of whether this is the last sentence-stress or not.

<u>Will</u> you drive to the óffice tomórrow?   (rather than the chauffeur)

<u>Will you</u> drive to the óffice tomórrow?   (rather than walk)

<u>Will you drive to the</u> óffice tomórrow?   (rather than anywhere else)

<u>Will you drive to the óffice to</u>mórrow? (rather than some other time)

<u>Will you</u> drive to the óffice to mórrow?   (no one idea singled out)

In the same way one idea can be singled out in a rising-falling pattern.

<u>It's my</u> bróther who néeds it.   (rather than I)

The need for thus singling out one idea in a thought group arises regularly in

1. *Making a question specific.*

<u>Was it</u> yóu who did thát?

<u>Whén do you</u> hópe to léave?

2. *Answering a specific question.*

(Who took the new car?)

I took the new cár.

(Did you take the new car, or leave it?)

I took the new cár.

(Did you take the new car, or the old one?)

I took the new cár.

3. *Contradicting an idea expressed elsewhere or merely implied.*

(He's not working hard.)

Yés, he is working hárd.

(Johnny will bring it to you.)

I wánt yóu to bring it to me.

(Will you please bring it here?)

Jóhnny will bring it to you.

I líke this récord.

But we dó belíeve you.

IV. Other Types of Intonation

There are many intonation patterns, other than those described in the last two lessons, which are at times used by native speakers of English. Thus, emotional emphasis may be expressed by the use of the slightly higher note in rising-falling intonation:

Thát's térrible!

A yes-no question may be given an added meaning of irony if it is pronounced with rising-falling intonation, like a statement of fact:

Do I knów him?   (He's my brother!)

A *wh*-question which is repeated (sometimes referred to as an "echo" question) has a rising intonation. The rise usually begins on the question word:

Whére does he líve?   (I didn't hear you.)

An authoritative work on the subject[4] describes thirty different "primary intonation contours." However, beyond the point reached in these two lessons, the principles become too complicated to be of much practical value to a foreign student of English; and they depend largely on mood and point of view, rather than grammatical construction and logic.

The simple types we have studied are sufficient, at the beginning, for normal conversational purposes. With them you can say almost anything in a natural and understandable way. Become as familiar with them as possible, and for a while try to use them for everything you say in English. Then, little by little, you can add new patterns—you will probably do so instinctively—by imitation.

---

[4] Kenneth L. Pike, *The Intonation of American English* (see note on p. 42).

Above all, do not make the mistake of thinking that all the various types of intonation you have been accustomed to using in your own language will have the same meaning if you transfer them to English. Many of your "intonation contours" do not exist in English, and others have entirely different meanings.

V. Exercises

A. Pronounce each group of sentences in the following exercise several times so as to accustom yourself to the various intonation patterns. Your instructor will try to see that you do not neglect to blend the words together smoothly.

1. <u>Do you remember me?</u>

2. <u>Is there a</u> róom for me?

3. <u>Do you have</u> ánything cheaper?

4. <u>Will you</u> kéep it lóng?

5. <u>Are you going to</u> stáy with us?

6. <u>Are you líving in</u> thís hotél?

7. <u>Is thát</u> Jóhn óver thére?

8. <u>Is</u> thís whére you éat?

9. <u>Will you</u> méet us thís évening?

10. <u>Is the</u> sécond flóor too lów for you?

11. You know it as well as I do.

12. The breakfasts are better than the dinners.

13. This room is more expensive than that one.

14. Yesterday's lecture was more interesting than today's.

15. John is older than Jim.

16. Have you met my wife, /Mr. Thomas?

17. Are you leaving now, /Miss Johnson?

18. Good morning, /Mr. Smith.

19. We'll see you later, /young man.

20. I'm glad to meet you, /Mrs. Smith.

21. What are you doing here, /William?

22. Where do you live, /Mr. Jackson?

23. My friend, /I want to tell you something.

24. Mr. Jackson,/this is Mrs. Smith.

25. You want a chair,/don't you?

26. It will be easier here,/won't it?

27. There's a pleasant breeze,/isn't there?

28. You have a beautiful view,/haven't you?

29. Shall we meet here,/or in the library?

30. Would you like a double room,/or a single one?

31. I saw Charles,/Robert,/and Harry.

32. It's open Monday,/Tuesday,/and Wednesday.

33. I can give you one at five,/six,/or seven dollars.

34. Boys often eat hamburgers;/men often eat steaks.

35. I say we do;/he says we don't.

36. This one is five;/that one is six.

37. If you wish,/I'll serve you now.

38. As you said,/it's a very nice place.

39. In a minute,/I'll have a surprise for you.

40. I looked down,/and there was my key.

41. It's unbelievable!

42. What a beautiful day!

43. What a strange sensation!

44. I never saw such a fool!

B. In order to improve your ability to control the ups and downs of your voice, to hear and produce an intonation pattern, it is suggested that a recording of Exercise A be made in class. As many students as possible should record groups of sentences, and these should be played back to the class immediately. The students will try to detect any failure to reproduce the pattern.

C. Read each of these sentences, first as a statement, then as a question, using only intonation to show the difference (see Section I of this lesson).

1. The story begins long ago.
2. They were riding in an old car.
3. The car began to cross the river.
4. The bridge had been washed away.

5. The children were in the back seat.

6. They were talking at the tops of their voices.

7. No one could hear anything.

8. One of the children fell out.

D. Pronounce each of the following questions in two ways: first, as if you were really asking for information; then, as if you knew the hearer would agree with you. After each reading of each sentence, another student should try to make the response which your intonation shows you expect of him. (See the end of Section II in this lesson.)

1. It's getting hotter, isn't it?

2. You don't think it will rain, do you?

3. It doesn't rain here in December, does it?

4. The nights are always warm, aren't they?

5. You can count on good weather in October, can't you?

6. The rainy season doesn't ever begin until winter, does it?

7. There's a lot of fog here, isn't there?

8. The mornings are warmer than the afternoons, aren't they?

9. The days are getting longer, aren't they?

10. Dinner is served at six o'clock, isn't it?

11. Concerts usually begin at eight o'clock, don't they?

12. They usually finish before eleven, don't they?

13. The library isn't open after midnight, is it?

14. The busses don't run on Sunday, do they?

15. The museum is open on Mondays, isn't it?

E. 1. By using the proper intonation, make this sentence, *I put my black coat away*, serve as an answer to each of the following questions (see Section III of this lesson).

a. What did you put away?

b. Where did you put your black coat?

c. Did the maid put your black coat away for you?

d. What coat did you put away?

e. Whose black coat did you put away?

2. Formulate a question which might result in each of the following answers.

a. She lost her handbag.

b. She lost her handbag.

c. She lost her handbag.

d. She lost her handbag.

3. Authors do not usually know anything about the theory of intonation, yet they frequently indicate by putting a word in italics that their sentences should be read with a certain intonation pattern. The lines below are taken from recent plays. How do you think the authors intended them to be spoken?

a. They don't want *me*.

b. *That's* a train trip for you.

c. I don't know *what* I'm going to do.

d. *Everybody* graduated this year.

e. We *don't* have to show you.

F. 1. The sentences below are to be marked for rhythm and intonation, and then read. A systematic way of analyzing material for this purpose is to

a. Mark all sentence-stresses. (In Part 1 of this exercise, all words may be stressed normally; there are no specially stressed function words.)

b. Divide into thought groups by placing a diagonal bar (/) at pauses. Be sure to mark as separate thought groups all (1) alternatives, (2) parts of a series, (3) words used in direct address, and (4) tag questions.

c. Mark the intonation of each group. First, locate the final high note or rise. (In Part 1 of this exercise, this may in all cases coincide with the last sentence-stress.) Second, determine whether the pattern should be rising-falling or rising, by deciding whether the group is a statement, command, *wh*-question, yes-no question, nonfinal group, or one of the special constructions listed in *b* above. Third, mark the intonation line from the final high note to the end of the group, distinguishing between shifts and glides. Fourth, decide whether or not you wish to give a high note to any nonfinal sentence-stresses, and mark such notes. Lastly, draw a line under the rest of the group, indicating normal pitch.

SENTENCES TO ANALYZE

1. Good morning, Miss Peterson. How are you feeling?

2. If it rains, we'll call off the whole thing.

3. You'll agree that it's the truth, won't you?

4. We are studying composition, pronunciation, and grammar.

5. There are two ways of accomplishing it: by kindness, or by threats.

6. He translates from English to French, and from French to English.

7. Which syllable is accented?

8. Miss Kim, will you open the door?

9.   Do you speak better than you read, or read better than you speak?

10.   Is the test on Monday or Tuesday?

2.   The sentences below are to be treated just as were those above. However, this second part of the exercise includes a few cases of specially stressed function words (see Lesson 4, end of Section II), and of final high notes which do not coincide with the last sentence-stress (see Section III of this lesson).

a.   It's not a large book, but a very small one.

b.   The class begins at four, and ends at five.

c.   A student may be good, bad, or indifferent.

d.   Do you want me, or him?

e.   Does he live on the left-hand side of the street?

f.   He lives on the right-hand side.

G.   Transcribe the following paragraph in phonetic symbols; then mark sentence-stresses, pauses, and intonation. After you have completed your analysis, your instructor will read the sentences, so that you can check your work with his pronunciation. It is not expected that each member of the class will mark the paragraph in exactly the same way. Finally, practice reading your corrected transcription.

1. Yes, dear, I know what I'm to bring home: bread, butter, and cheese.

2. It's written down here in my notebook, so I won't forget it.   3. Shall

I get a pound of butter, or half a pound?   4. What kind of butter do

you want?   5. As for me, I like local butter.   6. But I'm sure you want

Wisconsin butter, don't you?

H. Outside of class, read aloud several pages of simple conversational
    material (a modern play, if possible), concentrating your attention on
    the intonation of questions which begin with an interrogative word.

Classification of Consonants; the Endings -s and -ed

I. Voiced and Voiceless Sounds

An important way in which one speech sound may differ from another is in voicing or the lack of it. We say that a sound is *voiced* if *our vocal cords vibrate* as we pronounce it; a sound is *voiceless* if it is pronounced *without such vibration*. Press your thumb and forefinger lightly against the sides of your larynx (the central part of your throat, where sounds are made); then pronounce /z/ and /s/ alternately in imitation of your teacher. You should be able to feel the vibration of the vocal cords as you say /z/, and notice no vibration as you say /s/. In other words, /z/ is a voiced sound and /s/ is voiceless.

Now try pronouncing /š/ and /ž/. Which of the two sounds is voiced?

Another means of distinguishing the two types is to stop your ears as you pronounce the sounds aloud. In the case of voiced sounds, you should then be able to hear clearly the vibration of the vocal cords. You will hear nothing, except perhaps the rushing of the air, as you say the voiceless sounds.

THE VOICED CONSONANTS ARE

b	l	ŋ	v	z
d	m	r	w	ž
g	n	ð	y	dž

THE VOICELESS CONSONANTS ARE

f	k	s	t	hw
h	p	š	θ	tš

ALL VOWEL SOUNDS ARE VOICED

Do not try to memorize the above lists. It is much better to pronounce all the sounds to yourself, with fingers on throat or in ears, until you can tell instantly whether each one is voiced or voiceless.

You may have noticed that there are a number of pairs of consonants—such as /s/ and /z/, /š/ and /ž/—which seem to be very much alike except that one is voiced and the other voiceless. The consonants /b/ and /p/ form another such pair: both sounds are made in the same place (between the lips) and in the same manner (by closing the lips, then opening them to let the air escape explosively); but /b/ is pronounced with vibration of the vocal cords, and /p/ without vibration. We may say that /b/ is the voiced counterpart of /p/. How many more such pairs can you discover?

Pronounce a prolonged /v/. In the middle of the sound, without interrupting the flow of air through your mouth, make your vocal cords stop vibrating. What sound is left? What is the voiceless counterpart of /v/?

What happens if you stop the vibration of the vocal cords while pronouncing /m/? We may say, then, that /m/ has no voiceless counterpart in English. The same is true of /l/, /n/, /ŋ/, /r/, /w/, and /y/. On the other hand, there are no voiced sounds corresponding to /h/ and /hw/.

This leaves the following pairs:

/b, p/	/g, k/	/v, f/	/ž, š/
/d, t/	/ð, θ/	/z, s/	/dž, tš/

The first pair, /b/ and /p/, may be regarded as two parts of the same sound; so may /d/ and /t/, /g/ and /k/, etc. In each case, the first symbol represents the voiced half of the sound, the second symbol the voiceless half.

Since there is so little difference between /z/ and /s/, for example, it is extremely easy to make the error of pronouncing one in place of the other. In some languages, such as German, there are very few final voiced consonants. When speaking English, a person whose first language is German will therefore have a strong tendency to unvoice final consonants whenever possible. If he sees the word *bed*, he may think he pronounces it as /bɛd/, but to an American it will probably seem that he says /bɛt/. We shall speak of this problem again in later lessons.

II. Stops and Continuants, Sibilants

It is sometimes useful to classify consonants in a second way, as *stops* or *continuants*. A continuant is a sound—like /m/—which may be prolonged as long as the speaker has breath to pronounce it. A stop must be pronounced instantaneously, and cannot be held—like /t/.

Is /n/ a stop or a continuant? What is /s/? /k/? /b/? /f/?

Among the continuants, four consonants are known as sibilants, because of the hissing sound with which they are pronounced. These are /z/, /s/, /ž/, and /š/. Note that these four make up two voiced-voiceless pairs: /z, s/ and /ž, š/. The classification of sibilant is significant, as we shall see shortly, in determining the pronunciation of the ending -s, which is so frequently used in English.

III. Point of Articulation

We shall also need to be able to classify consonants in one other way, as to their *point of articulation*, or the place in the mouth where they are pronounced. Six of these points are shown in Figure 8.

If we begin at the front of the mouth and work back, we shall find first a group of three sounds made with *the lips*: /b/, /p/, and /m/. Try making them.

Between *the upper teeth and the lower lip*, we make two English sounds: /v/ and /f/.

By inserting the tongue *between the teeth*, we make /ð/ and /θ/.

By touching the tip of the tongue to *the tooth ridge* (just behind the upper teeth), we make four sounds: /d/, /t/, /n/, and /l/. In some other languages (French, Greek, Hebrew, Russian, etc.) these same sounds are pronounced with the tongue tip touching the upper teeth themselves.

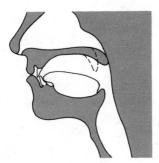

Lips, /b/, /p/, and /m/

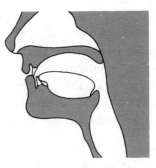

Upper teeth and lower lip,
/v/ and /f/

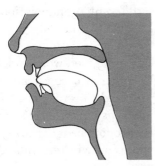

Between teeth, /ð/ and /θ/

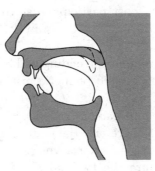

Tooth ridge, /d/, /t/, /n/, and /l/

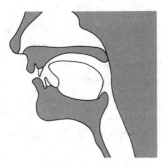

Passage between tongue and tooth
ridge, /z/, /s/, /ž/ and /š/

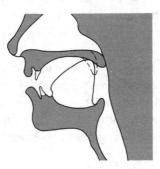

Roof of mouth, /g/, /k/, and / ŋ /

Figure 8. Points of articulation of consonants

By allowing the air to escape through *a narrow passage between the tongue and the tooth ridge*, we form /z/, /s/, /ž/, and /š/.

Pressing the back of the tongue against *the roof of the mouth*, we form /g/, /k/, and /ŋ/.

The points of articulation of the other consonants—/h/, /y/, /r/, /w/, /hw/, /tš/, and /dž/—will be described in later sections devoted specially to those sounds.

IV. Pronunciation of -ed

The ending -ed, added to regular English verbs to form the past tense and past participle, has three different pronunciations: /t/ as in *wished* /wišt/, /d/ as in *failed* /feyld/, and /ɪd/ as in *needed* /níydɪd/.

The sound the ending will have in any given word is determined by a very simple phonetic principle: when two consonants are pronounced together, as /r/ and /d/ in *cared* /kɛərd/, *it is difficult to voice one and leave the other voiceless, and easy to voice both or leave both voiceless.* Therefore, the ending -ed is pronounced /d/ after a voiced sound, and /t/ after a voiceless sound. You will remember that /d/ and /t/ are the two halves of a voiced-voiceless pair; in phonetic terms, this pair /d, t/ is the sign of the past tense and past participle.

How would the ending -ed be pronounced after a vowel? Remember that all vowels are voiced.

Suppose one now wishes to add the sound /d/ or /t/ to a word which already ends in one of those two sounds, in other words, to add /d, t/ to /d, t/. It is almost impossible to do so without inserting some sort of a vowel sound between the two consonants. Because vowels are voiced, the insertion of a vowel here means that the final d̲ will be pronounced as /d/ rather than /t/. In other words, after t̲ or d̲ the ending -ed is pronounced as a separate syllable, /ɪd/.

THE ENDING -ED IS PRONOUNCED

1. /d/ AFTER ALL VOICED CONSONANTS EXCEPT /d/, AND AFTER ALL VOWEL SOUNDS:
   planned /plænd/, judged /džədžd/, played /pleyd/
2. /t/ AFTER ALL VOICELESS CONSONANTS EXCEPT /t/:
   rocked /rakt/, kissed /kɪst/, ripped /rɪpt/
3. AS A SEPARATE SYLLABLE, /ɪd/, AFTER /d, t/:
   protected /prətɛ́ktɪd/, intended /ɪntɛ́ndɪd/

The most common errors which result from failure to observe the above principles are

1. The pronunciation of -ed as a separate syllable after consonants other than /d/ or /t/:

robbed as /rábɪd/, instead of /rabd/
thanked as /θǽŋkɪd/, instead of /θǽŋkt/

2. The pronunciation of -ed as /t/ after /l/, /r/, or a vowel:

dared as /dɛart/, instead of /dɛard/
killed as /kɪəlt/, instead of /kɪəld/

3. Apparent omission of the entire ending:
answered as /ǽnsər/, instead of /ǽnsərd/

There is only one type of exception to these rules, namely, a group of *adjectives* which end in -ed and therefore look like verbs: *ragged, wretched*, etc. Contrary to the principles outlined above, the ending of these words is pronounced as a separate syllable, /ɪd/: /rǽgɪd/, /rɛ́tšɪd/.

A *naked* /néykɪd/ child   A *two-legged* /túwlɛ̀gɪd/ animal

A *ragged* /rǽgɪd/ coat   A *wicked* /wíkɪd/ idea

The *rugged* /rə́gɪd/ rock   A *wretched* /rɛ́tšɪd/ day

An *aged* /éydžɪd/ minister (Compare: He has *aged* /eydžd/ a lot.)

The *blessed* /blɛ́sɪd/ virgin (Compare: The Pope *blessed* /blɛst/ the crowd.)

A *dogged* /dɔ́gɪd/ determination (Compare: The little boy *dogged* /dɔgd/ his brother's steps.)

V. Pronunciation of -s

In English, to make a noun plural or possessive, or to put a verb in the third person singular form of the present tense, we add /z, s/ to the end of the word. This ending is spelled in several different ways: -s (two hours, he says), -es (several churches, she kisses), -'s (a moment's time), or -s' (the grocers' prices). However it may be spelled, the ending is pronounced, according to strict phonetic principles, in one of three ways: /z/, /s/, or /ɪz/. The principles are the same as those which determine the pronunciation of -ed. Can you formulate them for yourself?

THE ENDING -s̲ (-ES̲, -'S̲, OR -S̲') IS PRONOUNCED

1. /z/ AFTER ALL VOICED CONSONANTS EXCEPT /z/ AND /ž/,
    AND AFTER ALL VOWEL SOUNDS:
    gam̲e̲s̲ /geymz̲/, call̲s̲ /kɔlz̲/, law̲s̲ /lɔz̲/
2. /s/ AFTER ALL VOICELESS CONSONANTS EXCEPT /s/ AND /š/:
    grant̲s̲ /grænts̲/, wrap̲s̲ /ræps̲/, Jack'̲s̲ /džæks̲/
3. AS A SEPARATE SYLLABLE, /ɪz/, AFTER A SIBILANT (/z, s/ or
    /ž, š/):
    dish̲e̲s̲ /díšɪz/, George'̲s̲ /džɔ́rdžɪz/, fox̲e̲s̲ /fáksɪz/

The above rules apply only when s̲ is added to a word as an
ending. If the final s̲ is a part of the basic word itself, as in *as, yes*,
etc., there is no logical way to decide whether it will be pronounced
/s/ or /z/. We must familiarize ourselves with the pronunciation of
each word individually. Here is a list of the most common such
words.

/z/		/s/	
as	/æz/	this	/ðɪs/
has	/hæz/	thus	/ðəs/
his	/hɪz/	us	/əs/
is	/ɪz/	yes	/yɛs/
was	/waz/ or /wəz/		

VI. Exercises

A. Are the following sounds voiced or voiceless? Divide them into two
    lists, and compare your results with the lists in Section I of this lesson.

1. f	8. w	15. k	22. tš
2. l	9. š	16. iy	23. p
3. t	10. r	17. ž	24. ð
4. b	11. dž	18. a	25. m
5. s	12. θ	19. d	26. h
6. n	13. v	20. y	27. ey
7. æ	14. ŋ	21. z	28. g

B. 1. What is the voiced counterpart of: š, f, k, tš, θ, p, s, t?
    2. How would a person with a German accent probably pronounce the
        underscored letters in this sentence (see Section I): "His̲ language
        show̲s̲ that he is̲ glad̲ to have̲ the job̲ and the big̲ salary that goes̲
        with it"?

C. Classify the following sounds as *voiced* or *voiceless, stop* or *continuant,* and give the *point of articulation* of each. For example, /d/ is a voiced stop, made with the tongue against the tooth ridge.

1.	v	4.	b	7.	n	10.	š	13.	ð
2.	p	5.	θ	8.	m	11.	d	14.	ž
3.	f	6.	s	9.	k	12.	z	15.	g

D. Suppose a student from Latin America pronounces the word *very* incorrectly, /bérɪ/ instead of /vérɪ/. Keeping in mind what you know about points of articulation, what would you tell him to do with his lips, teeth, etc., in order to change /b/ to /v/? How would you help a French student to say *think* as /θɪŋk/ instead of /sɪŋk/? *those* as /ðowz/ instead of /zowz/? A Chinese student to pronounce *man* as /mæn/ instead of /mæŋ/? A German student to pronounce *that* as /ðæt/ instead of /dæt/? A Scandinavian to say *thanks* as /θæŋks/ instead of /tæŋks/?

E. Pronounce each of these words, and write the phonetic symbol which represents the sound you gave to the ending. Then, in each case, explain why the ending is pronounced as it is.

1.	added	7.	longed	13.	believed	19.	wicked
2.	wished	8.	armed	14.	answered	20.	boxed
3.	caused	9.	aired	15.	showed	21.	lasted
4.	dropped	10.	asked	16.	lighted	22.	wretched
5.	crossed	11.	changed	17.	laughed	23.	learned
6.	robbed	12.	minded	18.	followed	24.	watched

25.	belongs	31.	bees	37.	ages	43.	acts
26.	bottoms	32.	bags	38.	blesses	44.	branches
27.	breaks	33.	attends	39.	articles	45.	caps
28.	bridges	34.	arrives	40.	chances	46.	confuses
29.	appears	35.	fixes	41.	cars	47.	armies
30.	allows	36.	chiefs	42.	America's	48.	animals

F. On page 81 of this lesson, you will find listed the three most common types of error made in pronouncing -ed. The errors made in pronouncing the ending -s, -es, etc., are fundamentally the same as items 2 and 3 on that list. Can you restate those two items in terms of -s, and give examples?

G.   Practice reading the following sentences at normal conversational speed. Be sure to pronounce the -s and -ed ending accurately.

While Ruth was washing the dishes one night, she cut her finger on a knife. She washed and bandaged it while her sister finished the dishes.

"I have two assignments to hand in tomorrow. I won't be able to type them very well now," Ruth complained.

Her sister stated emphatically, "Don't expect me to type your papers for you. I've got things of my own to do tonight."

"I'll give you the earrings I bought yesterday if you'll do it."

Ruth's sister laughed, but she refused to say anything.

"I'll make your bed for the rest of the week, too," promised Ruth.

Her sister smiled.

"You'll do it?" asked Ruth.

"Yes. You talked me into it," asnwered her sister, "but maybe I agreed too soon. Who knows what you might have promised if I had waited a little longer."

H.   Where would the high note or notes of the intonation pattern fall in the sentences below? In each of them the special attention of the hearer should be focused on one or two ideas, because of a comparison, contrast, contradiction, or a desire to make a question or an answer specific. (See Lesson 6, Section II, and the last part of Section III.) The sentences make up a connected passage, and should be considered in the light of what precedes and follows. Underline the syllables on which attention is to be focused, and then read the exercise with the proper intonation.

1.   Her composition is better than mine.
2.   Isn't his still better?
3.   No, I have a higher grade than he has.
4.   What grade did Robert get?
5.   He got an "A."
6.   No, he didn't get an "A."
7.   He got "C" on his paper.
8.   On the one he handed in this afternoon, or the one he handed in yesterday afternoon?
9.   The one he handed in this afternoon.
10. What was the subject of the paper?

I.　The passage which follows[1] has been transcribed in phonetic symbols, and marked for rhythm and intonation as an American might speak it. In other words, almost everything possible has been done so that your eye may help your ear and speech organs in pronouncing it. Read it several times, concentrating successively on (1) the sound of the symbols, (2) the regular return of sentence-stresses, (3) the intonation patterns, (4) combining all these elements. (If enough class time is available, this exercise might well be recorded.)

1. wɔ́ltər stápt ðə kár/ɪn frə́nt əv ðə bíəldɪŋ hwɛər hɪz wáyf wɛ́nt tə

hǽv hər hɛ́ər də́n.　2. "hwayl áym hǽvɪŋ may hɛ́ər də́n,/rɪmɛ́mbər tə

gɛ́t ðówz ówvəršùwz,"/šiy sɛ́d.　3. "ay downt níyd ówvəršùwz,"/sɛ́d

wɔ́ltər.　4. šiy pʊt hər mírər bǽk ɪntu hər bǽg.　5. "wiy dɪskə́st ɔ́l

ðǽt,"/šiy sɛ́d,/gɛtɪŋ áwt əv ðə kár.　6. "yuw arnt ə yə́ŋ mǽn ɛ́nɪ

lɔ́ŋgər."　7. hiy pʊ́št ðɪ ækséələrèytər dáwn/ən réyst ðə mówtər.

8. "hwáy downt yuw wɛ́ər yur glə́vz?"/šiy ǽskt.　9. "hǽv yu lɔ́st yur

glə́vz?"　10. wɔ́ltər ríytšt ɪn ə pákɪt/ən brɔt áwt ðə glə́vz.　11. hiy pʊt

ðəm án,/bət ǽfter šiy əd tə́rnd ən gɔ́n ɪntu ðə bíəldɪŋ/ən hiy əd drɪvən

án tu ə rɛ́d láyt,/hiy tʊk ðəm ɔ́f əgɛ́n.

J.　Read aloud several pages from a book you are studying, concentrating your attention on the pronunciation of the -s and -ed endings.

---

[1]Adapted from the story, "The Secret Life of Walter Mitty," by James Thurber, originally published in the *New Yorker*.

Initial and Final Consonants

I. The Aspiration of Initial Stop Consonants

In Lesson 7, we considered the eight pairs of consonants /b, p/, /d, t/, /g, k/, /ð, θ/, /v, f/, /z, s/, /ž, š/, and /dž, tš/. It was pointed out that, in each of these pairs, the first sound is very similar to the second, except that the one is voiced and the other is voiceless. The *chief difference*, then, between two words such as *big* /bɪg/ and *pig* /pɪg/ is that the initial consonant of *big* is pronounced with vibration of the vocal cords, and the initial consonant of *pig* without vibration.

However, that is not the only difference. Speakers of English have developed a *secondary type of difference* which occurs with the set of sounds which are called *stop consonants*: /b, p/, /d, t/, and /g, k/. When these sounds appear in initial position, the voiceless sound in each pair—/p/, /t/, /k/—is produced with a little puff of air, or—in more technical words—the initial voiceless stop sounds are aspirated. This principle may be stated as follows:

VOICELESS STOP CONSONANTS ARE ASPIRATED AT THE
BEGINNING OF A WORD.

In many other languages, initial voiceless stop consonants are not regularly aspirated, and people who learned one of these languages first usually find it hard to aspirate properly in English. For example, a Spanish-speaking student may seem to say, "I need the time" (/daym/ instead of /taym/). This pronunciation may lead to misunderstanding, and is certain to be noticed as an element of a "foreign accent." The student could correct his pronunciation by releasing the /t/ with a puff of air and without vibrating the vocal cords.

When we feel that it is important to show that a consonant is aspirated, we write a small h̲ above the line after the symbol: *time* /tʰaym/.[1]

Medial voiceless stops—those which occur within a word, after the first vowel sound and before the last—are aspirated in the same way when they appear at the beginning of a stressed syllable: *apartment* /əpʰártmənt/, *support* /səpʰɔ́rt/, *contain* /kəntʰéyn/. Others are not aspirated as strongly: *paper* /pʰéyp̱ər/, *taking* /tʰéyḵɪŋ/.

An exception among medial voiceless stops is a special type of /t/—one which occurs between voiced sounds, usually vowels, and does not stand at the beginning of a stressed syllable: for example, the t̲'s in *átom* and *húrting* (but not the t̲ in *áfter*, which stands between a voiceless and a voiced sound; nor that of *retéll*, which stands at the beginning of a stressed syllable). This sound is produced by a quick flap of the tongue against the tooth ridge with vocal cords vibrating. Many educated Americans appear to make no difference between this type of /t/ and a /d/. *Atom* /ǽtəm/ and *Adam* /ǽḏəm/ sound alike in their speech, and the hearer must rely on the meaning of the sentence in order to tell which is intended. It is probable, however, that many speakers do make a slight difference between the two sounds. Perhaps the best advice to a foreign student of English is to pronounce this special medial /t/ "somewhat like a /d/," without aspiration, and very rapidly: *butter* /bə́ṯər/, *pretty* /príṯɪ/, *forty* /fɔ́rṯɪ/.

II. The Lengthening of Vowels Before Final Consonants

Even more often than at the beginning of words, voiced consonants are confused with their voiceless counterparts at the end of words: *I live* (/lɪf̱/ instead of /lɪv̱/) *in California*, or *Who was* (/was̱/ instead of /waẕ/) *it?* In the speech of students of English, this type of error is probably more frequent than any other type, with the exception of the failure to give unstressed vowels their normal sound of /ə/ or /ɪ/.

---

[1]Phonetic markings such as this are introduced into an otherwise phonemically based notation only as pedagogical devices. (See Lesson 1, Section III.)

In doing the exercises of Lesson 7, you may have had great difficulty making a word like *years* sound like /yɪərz/ instead of /yɪərs̲/, even though you knew the final sound should be voiced, and tried hard to make your vocal cords vibrate as you pronounce it. The fact is that voicing or the lack of it is not the only difference between the /s/ and /z/ sounds at the end of a word. Just as in the case of the initial stop consonants, we do not rely on vibration of the vocal cords alone to distinguish a final voiced consonant from its voiceless counterpart.

There are at least three differences between the sound of *bus* /bəs̲/ and that of *buzz* /bəz̲/. The first is, of course, that /z/ is voiced, /s/ is voiceless. The second is that the vowel before /z/ is lengthened; it usually takes almost twice as long to say *buzz* as to say *bus*. The third difference—the more forceful articulation of the final /s/—will be discussed in Section III of this lesson.

When we feel it is important to show that a sound is lengthened, we place a colon (:) after it: *buzz* /bə:z/.

The second difference mentioned above between final /s/ and /z/ serves to distinguish all voiced consonants at the end of words from their voiceless counterparts; *bed* /bɛ:d/ takes longer to say than *bet* /bɛt/, *rib* /rɪ:b/ longer than *rip* /rɪp/, *bag* /bæ:g/ longer than *back* /bæk/.

BEFORE A FINAL VOICED CONSONANT, STRESSED VOWELS
ARE LENGTHENED.

If you will deliberately try to lengthen the vowel, it may be easier for you to make *years* sound like /yɪərz̲/ rather than /yɪərs̲/. This lengthening will increase the tendency toward diphthongization which is noticeable in many stressed English vowels.

III. Forceful Articulation of Consonants

The third difference between final /s/ and /z/, as in *bus* and *buzz*, is that /s/ is pronounced with a great deal of force, the /z/ with very little. In other words, at the end of /bəs/ a listener can hear very clearly the sound of air escaping through the teeth; at the end of /bəz/ there is much less sound of escaping air.

To sum up: if you find it hard to make a word like *years* sound like /yɪərz̲/ instead of /yɪərs̲/, the difficulty with /z/ may be overcome by trying consciously to

1.   Make your vocal cords vibrate to the very end of the word.

2. Lengthen the final vowel.

3. Allow very little sound of escaping air.

The forceful articulation which helps distinguish /s/ at the end of a word, however, is *not* typical of all other voiceless consonants in the same position. Usually it is heard only with final voiceless *continuants* (/f/, /θ/, /s/, /š/), not with final voiceless *stops* (/p/, /t/, /k/).

AT THE END OF A WORD, ONLY VOICELESS CONTINUANTS ARE PRONOUNCED WITH A GREAT DEAL OF FORCE.

Many students from abroad do, however, try to pronounce final consonants other than voiceless continuants with a great deal of force. This may sound like aspiration: an Italian may pronounce *I don't think so* as /ay downt^h θıŋk^h sow/. The little puffs of air after /t/ and /k/ sound like extra syllables. In extreme cases, the student may even add an /ə/ at the end of *don't* and *think* in order to pronounce the /t/ and /k/ more clearly: /ay downt^{h}ə θıŋk^{h}ə sow/. This, of course, completely destroys the natural rhythm of the sentence.

Normally, two movements are necessary for the production of a stop, such as /t/, /k/, or /p/. There is first a *closure,* or stopping of the outflow of air: for /t/, the tongue tip presses against the tooth ridge; for /k/, the back of the tongue rises and presses against the soft palate; for /p/, the lips are closed. As soon as a little pressure has been built up, comes the second movement, the *release* of the air: for /t/ the tongue tip leaves the tooth ridge; for /k/, the back of the tongue falls away from the soft palate; for /p/, the lips open. It is during this second movement that aspiration, the sound of escaping air, may be heard to a greater or lesser degree.

In conversational American English, there is such a powerful tendency to avoid the strong aspiration of final stop consonants that at the end of a word we regularly pronounce only the first half of a stop. *We make the closure, but allow our voice to die before the release.* If we say "A ship!" the sound ends while our lips are still pressed together for the /p/, and the lips may not open again for some time. If we say "You're right," we similarly avoid any "finishing sound" after /t/. It may seem to you that this would mean that the final /p/ or /t/ would simply not be heard. A native speaker of English, however, comes by long practice to be able to distinguish between final stops by the sound of their closure alone.

IV. Exercises

A. Summarize this lesson by writing *yes* or *no* after the questions in the following table, and by supplying additional examples.

TABLE OF DIFFERENCES BETWEEN VOICELESS AND
VOICED CONSONANTS IN VARIOUS POSITIONS

Between an initial voiceless consonant (like the /k/ in /<u>k</u>ud/) and its voiced counterpart (/<u>g</u>ud/):

	/<u>k</u>ud/	/<u>g</u>ud/
1. Is it voiced?	*yes* no	YES
2. Is it aspirated?	YES	no
Additional examples:	/_____/ and /_____/	
	/_____/ and /_____/	

Between a final voiceless stop and its voiced counterpart:

	/sæ<u>t</u>/	/sæ<u>d</u>/
1. Is it voiced?	no	YES
2. Preceding vowel lengthened?	no	YES
Additional examples:	/_____/ and /_____/	
	/_____/ and /_____/	

Between a final voiceless continuant and its voiced counterpart:

	/rey<u>s</u>/	/rey<u>z</u>/
1. Is it voiced?	*No*	*Yes*
2. Pronounced with great force?	*Yes*	*No*
3. Preceding vowel lengthened?	*No*	*Yes*

Additional examples: /_____/ and /_____/

/_____/ and /_____/

B. What advice (regarding aspiration, vowel length, voicing, and force of articulation) would you give a fellow student who made the following errors in pronunciation?

1. *had* as /hæ<u>t</u>/ instead of /hæ<u>d</u>/
2. *than* as /θæn/ instead of /ðæn/
3. *five* as /fay<u>f</u>/ instead of /fay<u>v</u>/
4. *dog* as /dɔ<u>k</u>/ instead of /dɔg/
5. *bus* as /bə<u>z</u>/ instead of /bə<u>s</u>/
6. *sing* as /zɪŋ/ instead of /sɪŋ/
7. *languages* as /lǽŋgwɪt̆šɪz/ instead of /lǽŋgwɪd̆žɪz/

C. Read each of the sentences below twice, using word (a) in the first reading and word (b) in the second. Then read again and use either (a) or (b), while another member of the class tries to identify in each case the word that you pronounced.

1. (a. back) (b. pack) Now I must go _____.
2. (a. bear) (b. pear) You can't eat a whole _____.
3. (a. mob) (b. mop) The leader kept the _____ well in hand.

4. (a. fast) (b. vast)   The patient has shown _____ improvement.

5. (a. feel) (b. veal)   He spoke on "The _____ of the Future."

6. (a. few) (b. view)   We saw a _____ on the hilltop.

7. (a. safe) (b. save)   Nothing will make a careless man _____.

8. (a. cold) (b. gold)   Are you getting _____?

9. (a. cave) (b. gave)   Under great pressure they _____ in.

10. (a. back) (b. bag)   Put your coat on your _____.

11. (a. dime) (b. time)   There's no _____ to lose.

12. (a. bed) (b. bet)   When he moved, he lost his _____.

13. (a. dead) (b. debt)   We must never forget the _____.

14. (a. feed) (b. feet)   He was off his _____.

15. (a. grade) (b. great)   The child was put in a _____ school.

16. (a. led) (b. let)   A traitor _____ the enemy in.

17. (a. seal) (b. zeal)   His _____ is well known.

18. (a. ice) (b. eyes)   You need good _____ to skate well.

19. (a. loss) (b. laws)   You can't avoid the _____ of the land.

20. (a. peace) (b. peas)   A meal without _____ is disappointing.

21. (a. place) (b. plays)   Put yourself in his _____.

22. (a. race) (b. raise)   I'll _____ you to the top.

23. (a. bridges) (b. breeches)   Don't burn your _____.

24. (a. ridge) (b. rich)   It was grown on _____ land.

25. (a. ether) (b. either)   The doctor wouldn't give her _____.

Your teacher may wish to use the above drill as a test of your ability to distinguish between voiced and voiceless sounds when you hear them. If so, take a piece of paper and number the lines from 1 through 25. The teacher will read each sentence, inserting one of the two test words. You should decide which one he used and write (a) or (b) on your paper opposite the number of the sentence.

D. There follows an exercise which will give you a chance to work on the special type of medial /t/ which is pronounced "somewhat like a /d/" (see end of Section I of this lesson). Remember that, in English, the tongue tip touches the tooth ridge rather than the upper teeth to form /t/ or /d/.

1. Read these sentences, paying particular attention to the underlined parts of the words.

   a. What's hur<u>t</u>ing you?

   b. She's ge<u>tt</u>ing the pota<u>t</u>oes.

   c. It's a pi<u>t</u>y you wai<u>t</u>ed so long.

   d. There's not enough wa<u>t</u>er to ma<u>tt</u>er.

   e. Be<u>tt</u>y wan<u>t</u>ed to stay la<u>t</u>er at the par<u>t</u>y.

   f. They have be<u>tt</u>er bu<u>tt</u>er at Ralph's.

2. Several members of the class should answer these questions by complete statements.

   a. At what age is a person at his best? (for<u>t</u>y, thir<u>t</u>y)?

   b. What girls do you think are pre<u>tt</u>y?

   c. What do you think of the a<u>t</u>om bomb?

   d. What kinds of foods (books, clothes, movies, music) do you like be<u>tt</u>er than others?

E. Using the words listed below describe some of the things that might happen in preparing for a picnic or that might take place on a picnic. This exercise is intended to give you practice in using aspirated consonants.

picnic	tennis	pear	basket	cold drinks
take	croquet	peach	people	table cloth
cook	tea	apple	towel	potato salad
plates	coffee	barbecue	park	potato chips
napkins	milk	pie	plan	clean
paper	cups	car	play	ice cream

F. Let the members of the class ask one another questions about their amusements, living arrangements, etc. Each question and answer should include the name (or a substitute for the name) of the person addressed: "Have you seen a good movie lately, Natalie?", "Oh yes, Mr. Liebmann, I saw a wonderful one last night." The instructor should listen carefully to see that proper intonation is used for direct address. (See Lesson 6, end of Section II.)

G. The sentences which follow were chosen because they contain a great many final voiced consonants. First find and draw a circle around all these final voiced consonants, and be sure that you understand the meaning of the passage. Then pronounce each sentence several times. If your teacher feels that any of the final voiced consonants sound like their voiceless counterparts, see what you can do to improve the pronunciation by more vibration of the vocal cords, a longer preceding vowel, and less forceful pronunciation.

1. ðə pleys ız kóld θríy rívərz,/bıkóz ıts lówkeytıd hwɛər ə léyk ız,

fórmd bay θríy stríymz.   2. ðɛər ər hándrədz əv kátıdžız an ðə šorz əv

ðə leyk.   3. ðə howtéəlz sárv vɛrı gúd míəlz.   4. džeymz əz spént fáyv

sámərz ðɛər/ən nówz évrıbədı.   5. durıŋ ðə déy hiy swímz;/æt náyt hiy

dǽnsız.   6. ðıs yíər hiy əz-téykən twéəlv dífrənt gárlz tə pártız.   7. hiy,

yúwzız hız fáðərz kár/ən əz lárnd tə dráyv ıt kwáyt wéəl.   8. ıf hız

frɛndz ər bórd,/hiy ólwız hæz bráyt aydíyəz fər θíŋz tə dúw.   9. hiy,

tráyz tə fərgét hız stádız,/ən névər ówpənz ə búk.   10. hiy fíəlz ðət,

veykéyšənz šud biy sɛvrəl yíərz lóŋ.

L, R, and Syllabic Consonants

I. The Formation of /l/ and /r/

Phoneticians sometimes classify /l/ and /r/ as glides. Other consonants are made with the speech organs in a more or less fixed position, but glides are characterized by the fact that they are formed as the organs of speech move from one place to another. Thus /w/, another glide, is begun with the lips protruding and rounded, and is pronounced as the lips move from this position to the position required for whatever vowel sound may follow the /w/.

Speakers of English normally pronounce /l/ with the tip of the tongue touching the *tooth ridge*, just behind the upper teeth. Note that in many other languages /l/ is made with the tongue tip touching the upper teeth themselves. The English /l/ also differs in that the middle of the tongue is usually lower in the mouth. *It is important to remember that the sides of the tongue do not touch anything;* the air goes out over both sides. If /l/ follows a vowel, as in *call* /kɔl/, the tongue, lips, etc., move from the position of the vowel to the /l/-position. The movement involves lowering the middle of the tongue in varying degrees, and then reaching for the tooth ridge with the tongue tip. During this motion, the vocal cords vibrate continuously, since /l/ is a voiced sound. It is the movement from one position to another which determines the characteristic sound of /l/. If the /l/ precedes a vowel, as in *lie* /lay/, the sound begins with the tongue tip already in position, and the middle of the tongue is not so low.

Pronounce *coal* /kowl/, *fool* /fuwl/, *pull* /pʊl/, *like* /layk/, *long* /lɔŋ/, being certain that your speech organs take the proper positions.

The /r/-sound is somewhat more complex. In certain parts of England, and the East and South of the United States, the sound hardly seems to be pronounced at all except at the beginning of a word or syllable. A large majority of English-speaking people, however, pronounce it with both sides of the tongue touching the back part of the tooth ridge and the back teeth. *It is important to note that the tongue tip does not touch anything;* the middle of the tongue, including the tip, is lower than the sides, and the air goes out through the channel formed between the middle of the tongue and the roof of the mouth. The lips are slightly open. The glide, the characteristic /r/-sound, is produced as the speech organs move to this position from a vowel, as in *are* /ar/, or away from this position to a vowel, as in *red* /rɛd/. In whatever direction the movement may end, *it always begins by a motion toward the back of the mouth.* More than any other factor, it is this retroflex (toward the back) motion that gives the English /r/ its typical sound. The tongue tip rises a little and is curved backward, while the sides of the tongue slide along the back part of the tooth ridge as along two rails.

Pronounce the vowel /a/. As you do so, curve the tip of your tongue up and slide the sides of the tongue backward along the tooth ridge, and you should have no difficulty in producing a perfect American /r/.

When /r/ follows a vowel, *or* /ɔr/, the entire movement is in a backward direction. When /r/ precedes a vowel, *right* /rayt/, the backward movement is very brief, and is almost immediately reversed as the tongue moves forward again to the vowel position. In addition, the lips are rounded. Note this as your teacher pronounces *right, ray, red.*

Many speakers of German, French, and certain other languages use a "uvular" r̠, made by vibrating the uvula (the little flap of flesh which hangs down at the entrance of the throat) or by the friction produced as the air passes between the uvula and the raised back portion of the tongue. This type of r̠ is also a glide, characterized by movement of the speech organs, but to produce it the tongue slides a little forward, rather than backward, and the muscles of the soft palate are tensed. Students who find it difficult to avoid this type of r̠ in English should concentrate on the *backward* movement of the tongue and making the uvula and soft palate (the soft back part of the roof of the mouth) remain motionless and relaxed.

The trilled r̲, typical of such languages as Spanish and Italian, can best be avoided by concentrating on the sliding of the sides of the tongue along the tooth ridge, by keeping the tongue tip comparatively inactive, and by being very careful that the tip does not approach closely the roof of the mouth or upper teeth.

Japanese and Chinese students, in particular, sometimes have difficulty in distinguishing between /l/ and /r/. They should spend a great deal of time pronouncing such pairs of words as *grass* /græs/ and *glass* /glæs/, *crime* /kraym/ and *climb* /klaym/, *free* /friy/ and *flee* /fliy/, *red* /rɛd/ and *led* /lɛd/, making the tip of the tongue touch the tooth ridge for /l/ and stay away from the roof of the mouth and teeth for /r/. In a sense, /l/ and /r/ are made in exactly opposite ways: for /l/ the tongue tip touches the tooth ridge and the air goes out over the sides; for /r/ the sides of the tongue touch the tooth ridge while the air goes out over the middle and tip.

II. /l/ and /r/ after Front Vowels

In Lesson 2 we learned to classify /iy/, /ɪ/, /ey/, /ɛ/, and /æ/ as front vowels; /ɔ/, /ow/, /ʊ/, and /uw/ as back vowels; and /a/ and /ə/ as central vowels. If the reasons for this classification are not clear to you now, it might be well to review that lesson at this point.

Both /l/ and /r/ are produced rather far back in the mouth; they are nearer the back vowels than the front vowels. As a result, it is a more complicated process and takes more time to pass from a front vowel to /l/ or /r/ than from a back vowel to these consonants. Compare *ill* and *all*, *ear* and *or*. As the speech organs move back from the position of the front vowel, they pass through the middle, central zone where /ə/ is formed. We may say then that

WHEN A FRONT VOWEL IS FOLLOWED BY /l/ OR /r/,
AN INTERMEDIARY /ə/ IS INSERTED.

No such /ə/ appears between a back vowel and /l/ or /r/, since the movement begins and ends in the back of the mouth without passing through the central zone. No such /ə/ is necessary between /a/ and /l/ or /r/ because /a/ is already produced with the tongue in central position. We pronounce *wall* as /wɔl/, but *well* as /wɛə̲l/.

In the same way, among words in which /r/ follows a vowel, we hear *car* /kar/ without the intermediary sound, and *care* /kɛə̱r/ with it.

The deliberate insertion of /ə/ in the cases just described will usually help a foreign student to produce an /l/ and /r/ which "sound American," and will enable him to avoid pronouncing such words as *will*, *bell*, and *feel* with an unnaturally pure vowel and with the tongue unnaturally high. The mispronunciation of words like these is a prominent feature of many a foreign accent. Think of them as /wɪə̱l/, /bɛə̱l/, and /fiə̱l/, rather than as /wɪl/, /bɛl/, and /fiyl/.

No /ə/ is inserted in words like *hilly* /hɪ́lɪ/, in which the /l/ is followed by another vowel sound, as it is in words such as *hill* /hɪə̱l/, in which the /l/ is final or followed by another consonant sound. The same is true for words with /r/: *merry* /mɛ́rɪ/, without /ə/; but *where* /hwɛə̱r/, with /ə/.

III. Syllabic Consonants

Most of us are accustomed to thinking that every syllable must include at least one vowel, yet in words such as *little*, *sudden*, and *wouldn't* there are only consonant sounds in the final syllable. These are known as syllabic consonants, since they may make up a syllable without the accompaniment of vowels. In phonetic transcription, syllabic consonants are indicated by drawing a short vertical line below them: *little* /lɪtl̩/, *sudden* /sədn̩/, *wouldn't* /wʊdn̩t/. They are difficult for most foreign students to pronounce; in place of /lɪtl̩/ we frequently hear /lɪtəl/ or /lɪl/; in place of /wʊdn̩t/ the student may say /wʊdənt/ or /wʊnt/.

Syllabic consonants occur when a syllable ends in /t/, /d/, or /n/, and the next syllable is *un*stressed and contains an /l/ or /n/. This may be expressed by an equation:

$$\left.\begin{matrix} t \\ d \\ n \end{matrix}\right\} + \text{unstressed syllable containing} \left\{\begin{matrix} l \\ n \end{matrix}\right. > \text{syllabic consonant.}$$

All the necessary conditions are present, for example, in *saddle* and *cotton*, and we have the pronunciations /sædl̩/ and /katn̩/. In *lieutenant* /luwtɛ́nənt/, there is a /t/ followed by an /n/, but the /n/ is in a stressed syllable, so no syllabic consonant results.

It is easy to remember the four consonants which are involved in syllabic consonants: /t/, /d/, /n/, and /l/. They are the four which are formed with the tip of the tongue touching the tooth ridge.[1] Indeed, it is the fact that the four are all made with the tongue tip in the same position that causes the formation of syllabic consonants. What happens is that, in pronouncing *cotton*, for example, the tongue tip goes to the tooth ridge to form /t/, *and just stays there to pronounce the following* /n/. There should not even be a brief separation of tip and tooth ridge between /t/ and /n/. If the tongue tip breaks contact and moves from its fixed position for even a fraction of a second, it will result in the insertion of an /ə/ between the two consonants. In a word such as *cotton*, an /ə/ in the second syllable is definitely an element of "foreign accent."

You will remember that the formation of a stop, like /t/ or /d/, usually requires two movements: a *closure*, or stopping of the outflow of air, and then a *release* of the air (see Lesson 8, Section III). Before a syllabic consonant, in words like *little* and *sudden*, the closure for the stop takes place normally, as the tongue tip makes contact with the tooth ridge. But the release is quite unusual, since the tongue tip, which normally makes the release by moving away from the tooth ridge, must in this case remain in its position for the formation of the following syllabic consonant. Before syllabic /l/ the release is made by a sudden lowering of the *middle and sides*—not the *tip*—of the tongue; this permits the air imprisoned by the preceding closure to rush out and make an /l̩/. Before syllabic /n/ the release is made by a sudden opening of the velum, which allows the imprisoned air to escape through the nose. (The velum is the soft part of the palate, at the back of the roof of the mouth. When drawn up, it closes the nasal passages, and all escaping breath must come out through the mouth; when relaxed and open, the breath may come out through either nose or mouth. See Figure 8, p. 79.)

So, when you wish to pronounce a word like *little* /lɪtl̩/ or *sudden* /sədn̩/, bring the tongue into contact with the tooth ridge sharply and definitely for the /t/ or /d/. Then, *as you force the tongue tip to remain where it is*, make the release which will produce

---

[1]In rapid conversational speech, syllabic consonants may occur in two other cases where stops and continuants have the same points of articulation: (1) between /p/ or /b/ and /m/, as in *stop 'em* /stapm̩/; and (2) between /k/ or /g/ and /ŋ/, as in *I can go* /aykŋgow/. Since the alternate pronunciations, /stapəm/ and /aykəngow/ do not sound "foreign," these two cases are not important for the purposes of this text. Some phoneticians also transcribe as syllabic consonants such combinations as the /l/ after the /s/ in *pencil*, /pɛnsəl/ or /pɛnsl̩/, and the /l/ after the /p/ in *apple*, /æpəl/ or /æpl̩/, where the points of articulation are not quite identical. In these cases also, however, either alternate pronunciation is perfectly normal American English.

/l/ or /n/. You may find it helpful at the beginning to pronounce the first syllable completely, /lɪt/, and to pause on the /t/ in order to feel and maintain the pressure of the tongue tip in its proper position before you go on to make the release and pronounce the last syllable, /l̩/. In the same way, try *important;* /ɪmpórt/, pause, /ṇt/; and *sentence,* /sɛnt/, pause, /ṇs/.

It should be noted that the /t/ which precedes a syllabic /l/, as in *little*, is the "/d/-like /t/" discussed at the end of Section I, Lesson 8.

IV. Exercises

A. This drill is intended to furnish you with an opportunity for extensive and careful practice in the correct formation of /r/. It begins with the combinations in which most students usually find it easiest to make an American /r/, and then moves on to more difficult combinations. Pronounce each item three or four times, more if necessary, keeping in mind the instructions given in Section I. Try to master each step in the exercise before you go on to the next one. Start with (a), then proceed to (b), etc.

	(a)		(b)		(c)
1.	ar	1.	kar	1.	farm
2.	ɔr	2.	fɔr	2.	bɜrn
3.	ɪər	3.	sɜr	3.	gɜrl
4.	ɛər	4.	hɪər	4.	mə́ðər
5.	ər	5.	ðɛər	5.	fáðər

	(d)		(e)		(f)
1.	mɔ́rnɪŋ	1.	ara	1.	mɛ́rɪ
2.	bárgɪn	2.	arow	2.	kǽrɪ
3.	wɜrk	3.	ariy	3.	mɔ́rəl
4.	wɔ́rmər	4.	ərə	4.	fyúrɪ
5.	bɔ́rdər	5.	ɔrɛ	5.	ɛ́rər

	(g)		(h)		(i)
1.	riy	1.	rɪd	1.	rəf
2.	rey	2.	reyn	2.	rowl
3.	ra	3.	rɛk	3.	rayd
4.	row	4.	rǽpɪŋ	4.	rawz
5.	ruw	5.	rɪfə́r	5.	rúwlər

(j)	(k)	(l)
1. gruw	1. θrown	1. ˊɛvrɪ
2. frow	2. brɪŋ	2. əpréyz
3. drɔ	3. kreyt	3. bɪfrɛ́nd
4. prey	4. prɪpér	4. dɪkríys
5. triy	5. gráwndɪd	5. bɪgrədž

(m)
1. a large farm
2. shorter working hours
3. to further your purposes
4. forever and ever
5. the wrong room

(n)
1. a greater artist
2. frequent arrivals
3. to cross the border
4. a brown dress
5. to bring under control

B. Your instructor will pronounce the following geographical names with an "American accent." Imitate him as closely as possible, paying special attention to the formation of /r/.

1.	Berlin	8.	Ferrara	15.	Rio de Janeiro
2.	Turkey	9.	Prague	16.	Cairo
3.	Hiroshima	10.	Tripoli	17.	Paris
4.	Peru	11.	Burma	18.	Rumania
5.	Smyrna	12.	Florida	19.	Warsaw
6.	Florence	13.	Madras	20.	France
7.	Karachi	14.	Teheran	21.	Argentina

C. These two exercises are particularly for Oriental students.

1. Pronounce each pair of words several times, remembering the differences between /l/ and /r/ as described in the last paragraph of Section I. In each case the two words sound exactly alike, except for /l/ and /r/.[2]

a.	late, rate	e.	alive, arrive	i.	believe, bereave
b.	cloud, crowd	f.	liver, river	j.	blight, right
c.	glue, grew	g.	play, pray	k.	blush, brush
d.	lime, rhyme	h.	glass, grass	l.	fly, fry

---

[2]Note to the teacher: In order to maintain a minimal distinction between the two words, help the students to pronounce each word with the same intonation: late–rate (rather than with a series intonation: late, rate).

2. Read the following paragraph, and then tell a fellow student what happened to Richard and Grace Robinson.

> Richard and Grace Robinson planned to attend a Broadway play while they were in New York. The traffic that night was very heavy, so they were late getting to the theatre. Because they arrived late, the usher told them they would have to stand at the rear of the auditorium until the end of the first scene. The play was so bad that they decided to leave. Since it was really too late to go anywhere else, they went back to the hotel and watched television.

D. In the light of what you learned in Section II of this lesson, determine which of the following words would be pronounced with an /ə/ inserted between the vowel sound and /l/ or /r/. Then transcribe all the words in phonetic symbols, and check them with your instructor's transcription. Finally, pronounce your transcriptions, taking particular care with combinations such as *well*, in which a front vowel precedes /l/.

1. bar	11. sir	21. full
2. for	12. word	22. milk
3. hair	13. heard	23. fell
4. ear	14. verb	24. ball
5. care	15. will	25. shall
6. beer	16. tell	26. help
7. bear	17. coal	27. pool
8. they're	18. kill	28. spelled
9. we're	19. real	29. failed
10. fur	20. self	30. she'll

E. Three of the words in the following exercise cannot contain syllabic consonants, but all the others can. Which are the three exceptions? Draw a line under the syllabic consonants in the other twenty-nine words (see Section III); then pronounce the entire exercise. Your instructor should pronounce this material with you, before you try to work on it alone.

1. little	8. harden	15. oriental
2. didn't	9. idle	16. bottle
3. student	10. important	17. saddled
4. couldn't	11. mountain	18. broadened
5. article	12. hospital	19. attention
6. tunnel	13. travel	20. battleship
7. Latin	14. curtain	21. suddenly

22. sentences	26. finally	30. monotonous
23. gardening	27. fertilize	31. bread and butter
24. certainty	28. ordinary	32. bright and early
25. penalty	29. ventilate	33. salt and pepper

F. Practice the following exercise several times, concentrating your attention on a different feature at each reading: (1) intonation, (2) the correct formation of /r/, (3) inserting an /ə/ between front vowels and /l/, (4) syllabic consonants, (5) the correct pronunciation of -s and -ed endings.

1. Bill likes nothing so well as mountain climbing.   2. He will tell you how important it is to start early.   3. If he doesn't feel like walking, he ordinarily rides a brown horse.   4. The trail is easier when dry weather has hardened the ground.   5. As he climbs, he rests very little until he has reached the top.   6. The clouds hang like a curtain over the river below him.   7. The horse looks in the brush for green grass.

8. Bill likes to leave the trail and ride right down the mountainside.

9. Once he fell and hurt his ankle; he still limps a little.   10. But Bill didn't tell anyone a word about it when he finally arrived back home.

11. Some day he'll kill himself or end up in the hospital.   12. I wouldn't care for anything so strenuous and risky myself.   13. I prefer gardening,

but Bill finds it a little monotonous.   14. I certainly couldn't get up,

so bright and early in the morning.   15. I must be paying the penalty,

of idleness; that's the real reason.

G. 1. As you answer these questions, use the intonation which is normal for a series (see Lesson 6, end of Section II).

a. What do you usually eat for breakfast?
b. What languages do you speak?
c. What courses are you taking now?
d. What countries have you visited?
e. What kinds of ice cream have you tried in this country?

2. Make questions in which you present the following ideas as alternatives with *or*; for example, "Is the food better in the *United States*, or in *your native country?*" Be careful with the intonation of the questions (see Lesson 6, end of Section II).

a. interesting, boring   f. January, June
b. a real fire, a false alarm   g. morning, afternoon
c. just beginning, ending   h. long, short
d. this school, the school you last attended i. easy, difficult
e. Monday, Tuesday, Wednesday   j. music, art

H. This lesson ends with a speed and rhythm drill. Read it at normal conversational speed, and try to observe an even, regular sentence rhythm (see Lesson 4, Section I). The material is well suited for individual laboratory work.

1. a. I fóund it.
    b. I've tóld you I fóund it.
    c. I've tóld you alréady that I fóund it.
    d. I've tóld you alréady that I fóund it at the móvies.
    e. I've tóld you alréady that I fóund the móney at the móvies.
    f. I've tóld you alréady that I fóund the móney at the móvies on Súnday.

2. a. I'm surprísed!

    b. I'm surprísed you belíeve it!

    c. I'm surprísed you belíeved such a stóry!

    d. I'm surprísed you belíeved such an incrédible stóry!

    e. I'm surprísed that ányone belíeved such an incrédible stóry!

    f. I'm surprísed that ányone belíeved such an incrédible stóry as thát!

3. a. He knóws éverything.

    b. He appéars to knów éverything.

    c. He sómetimes appéars to knów éverything.

    d. He sómetimes appéars to knów éverything when he léctures.

    e. He sómetimes appéars to knów éverything when he léctures so cónfidently.

    f. He sómetimes appéars to knów éverything when he léctures so cónfidently to his clásses.

I. Outside of class, read aloud several pages of simple, conversational material, concentrating your attention on the pronunciation of /l/, or /r/, whichever seems to give you most trouble.

Front Vowels

I. Vowel Substitutions

A common—and very serious—mistake made by students of English is the substitution of one vowel for another in the stressed syllable of a word: for example, the pronunciation of *leaving* as /lívɪŋ/ instead of /líyvɪŋ/. Such a substitution is serious because it often completely changes the meaning of the word. It may be polite to tell your friend, "/ay howp yuw wownt liyv naw/"; but "/ay howp yuw wownt lɪv naw/" may not be appreciated.

The usual causes for mistakes of this sort seem to be

1. The speaker gives the letters which represent vowels the sounds these letters would have in his native language. A Frenchman tends to pronounce *aid* as /ɛd/ instead of /eyd/.

2. The speaker is deceived by the inconsistencies of English spelling. Usually ar is pronounced /ar/, as in *car, far,* and *part;* therefore *war* is sometimes wrongly pronounced as /war/ instead of /wɔr/.

3. The speaker cannot hear, and consequently cannot reproduce, the difference between two sounds, either because the two do not exist in his own language, or because they never serve to distinguish between words in it. Both /ey/ and /ɛ/ are heard in Spanish, but there are no two Spanish words which are exactly

alike except that one contains /ey/ and the other /ɛ/. As a result, the student from Mexico often mispronounces *change* as /tšɛndž/ instead of /tšeyndž/.

Lessons 10, 11, 12, and 13 attack the problem of stressed vowel substitutions. They are intended to give you practice in hearing and reproducing the differences between vowels which are frequently confused, to give you an opportunity to make stronger associations between vowel sounds and their usual spelling, and to call your attention to certain common words in which the vowel sounds are spelled in an unusual way.

II. The Vowel /iy/ as in b**ea**t

The material which follows is based on the vowel chart as explained in Lesson 2. (It would be well at this point to review that explanation, see particularly Figure 3 on page 13.)

You may remember that /iy/ is the vowel which is pronounced farthest toward the front of the mouth, with the jaw nearly closed. *The sides of the tongue are pressed tightly against the upper bicuspid (two-pointed) teeth and the palate (roof of the mouth).* The tongue tip may *press the cutting edge* of the lower front teeth. *Upper and lower teeth almost touch. The lips are spread somewhat by muscular force. The air escapes through a very narrow opening between the tongue blade (the part just behind the tip) and the upper tooth ridge.* In general, /iy/ is made with a great deal of tension and effort. Although the tongue is already very high in the front of the mouth when you begin this sound, the tongue sometimes moves farther up before beginning the next sound; therefore, this sound is symbolized as a vowel plus a glide: /iy/.

This is the vowel heard in *she* /šiy/, *seem* /siym/, *leave* /liyv/, *chief* /tšiyf/, etc. Say these words carefully after your teacher, then pronounce the vowel in each of them alone: /šiy/, /iy/; /siym/, /iy/; etc. As you pronounce, make sure that your tongue, teeth, and lips take the position described in the preceding paragraph.

III. /ɪ/ as in b**i**t

The vowel which follows /iy/ on the vowel chart, as we move away from the front of the mouth, is /ɪ/. To change /iy/ to /ɪ/, *the jaw relaxes and drops very slightly, the pressure of the sides of the tongue against the upper bicuspids decreases, and the forced spreading of the lips disappears.* The tongue tip may merely *touch the back* of the lower front teeth. To see clearly what happens to lips, jaws, and tongue, it is best to watch your mouth in a hand mirror as you form /iy/ and /ɪ/. *Most important of all, the opening between the tongue blade and the palate becomes wider and rounder.* This means that the place where the tongue and palate are closest together moves a little farther back in the mouth.

Pronounce *sheep* /šiyp/, then *ship* /šɪp/, in imitation of your teacher. Now pronounce just the vowels of the two words: /iy/, /ɪ/, /iy/, /ɪ/, /iy/, /ɪ/. Can you feel the essential differences in the position of the speech organs clearly? Form an /iy/-sound; then without interrupting the flow of breath, try to make the /iy/ change to an /ɪ/ by appropriate movements of the tongue, jaw, and lips.

The /ɪ/-sound is the vowel of *big* /bɪg/, *king* /kɪŋ/, and *city* /sítɪ/. In some languages this sound does not exist. In others it may be heard occasionally, but does not differentiate words from similar words containing /iy/. Students who learned these other languages first will probably have difficulty in distinguishing clearly between *leave* /liyv/ and *live* /lɪv/. Very often they will use, instead of /iy/ or /ɪ/, a vowel halfway between the two, which will make *leave* sound like *live*, or *live* like *leave*, to an American ear.

The use of /iy/ for /ɪ/ or of /ɪ/ for /iy/ is, in fact, by far the most common and troublesome of the vowel substitutions we spoke of at the beginning of this lesson.

IV. /ey/ as in ba̲i̲t

Moving downward and backward on the vowel chart from /ɪ/, we come to /ey/. *The jaw drops just a little more.* The tongue tip may touch the *bottom* of the front teeth without pressure. *The sides of the tongue press slightly against the sides of the upper bicuspids. The passage through which the air escapes between the middle of the tongue and the palate grows wider. The lips are open and relaxed.*

Perhaps the characteristic which best distinguishes /ey/ is that *it is pronounced with a definite upward and forward movement of the tongue.* The complete vowel begins in the position described in the preceding paragraph, then moves upward and forward toward the /ɪ/ position as the tongue is pushed nearer the palate and upper front teeth. The diphthongization of /ey/ is much more discernible than that of /iy/, and it is also much greater in most varieties of British English than in American English.

The degree of diphthongization is greatest in words where /ey/ is:

1. Followed by a final voiced consonant: *made* /meyd/.

2. Final: *day* /dey/.

3. Pronounced with a glide at the end of an intonation pattern:

<u>It's the hand of fate.</u>   /ɪts ðə hænd əv feyt/

The /ey/-sound is the vowel heard in *say* /sey/, *plain* /pleyn/, and *came* /keym/. It is most often confused with /ɛ/ and /æ/. Can you see the difference between /ey/, /ɪ/, and /iy/ in your mirror?

V. /ɛ/ **as in b<u>e</u>t**

After /ey/ on the chart comes /ɛ/; but unlike /ey/, /ɛ/ is not usually diphthongized. To form /ɛ/, *the jaw is once more lowered just a little. For the first time, the tongue exerts no pressure at all.* The tongue tip may touch the spot where the lower front teeth join the tooth ridge; *the sides touch the tips of the upper bicuspids. The air-escape passage is as wide as the roof of the mouth itself.*

The /ɛ/-sound is the vowel of *yes* /yɛs/, *edge* /ɛdž/, and *end* /ɛnd/. It is not as clear a sound as /ey/, from which it must be carefully distinguished. Make sure you have understood and seen the chief differences: /ɛ/ is not diphthongized, and in forming it the sides of the tongue touch lightly the tips of the upper bicuspids without pressure. For /ey/ there is enough pressure to narrow the air passage somewhat.

VI. /æ/ **as in b<u>a</u>t**

The last of the front vowels is /æ/. *To form it the jaw is lowered quite a bit, until the mouth is almost as wide open as it can be without making a muscular effort.* Remember that this is the last front vowel that can be made; when we move on to /a/, the sides and tip of the tongue will no longer touch the upper or lower teeth at all. *For /æ/, the lightest possible contact is made between tongue tip and lower tooth ridge, and between sides of tongue and the tips of the upper bicuspids or even of the first molar teeth just behind the bicuspids.* In other words, the passage through which the air escapes is as wide and deep as it can be and still remain a passage formed by the tongue rather than by the cheeks.

The /æ/-sound is the vowel of *am* /æm/, *black* /blæk/, and *cap* /kæp/. It is easily confused with /a/, /ɛ/, or even /ey/. Before you go on to the next section of this lesson, it would be well to go over the entire series—/iy-ɪ-ey-ɛ-æ/—many times with your mirror, checking your way of forming the sounds with the physiological descriptions of how they should be formed.

VII. Exercises

A. 1. Listen carefully to your instructor as he pronounces a prolonged /iy/ several times: /iy—, iy—, iy—/. Imitate his pronunciation of the vowel, watching your lips, tongue, teeth, etc., in a hand mirror and trying to make your speech organs assume the exact position described in the appropriate section of this lesson.

2. Listen, then imitate, as your instructor pronounces the following material. Finally, try to pronounce each word or phrase to his satisfaction. If he finds that the vowel in any word does not sound quite right, correct yourself by making your speech organs assume more exactly the desired position.

(a)	(b)	(c)
1. biy	1. these dreams	1. riyd, rɪd
2. miy	2. green trees	2. hiyt, hɪt
3. friy	3. weak tea	3. sliyp, slɪp
4. iytš	4. meet in the street	4. miyt, mɪt
5. iyst	5. please teach me	5. fiyd, fɛd
6. šiyp	6. a deep sleep	6. siyt, sɛt
7. siyk		
8. niyd		
9. fiyt		
10. kwiyn		

B. The instructions for Exercise A apply also to Exercises B, C, D, and E.

1. /ɪ—, ɪ—, ɪ—/

2.

(a)	(b)	(c)
1. bɪt	1. this city	1. sɪt, siyt
2. fɪks	2. a quick finish	2. lɪp, liyp
3. kɪs	3. which gift	3. stɪk, steyk
4. rɪŋ	4. six inches	4. mɪs, mɛs
5. trɪp	5. to visit my sister	5. sɪns, sɛns
6. wɪn	6. spill the milk	6. hɪm, hɛm
7. lɪft		
8. ɪts		
9. ɪf		
10. ɪŋk		

C. 1. /ey—, ey—, ey—/

2.   (a)   (b)   (c)
    1. pey   1. straight pay   1. pleyn, plæn
    2. sey   2. a date at eight   2. greys, græs
    3. grey   3. a famous flavor   3. geyt, gɛt
    4. eyt   4. the baby's name   4. bleyd, blɛd
    5. eydž   5. made me late   5. teyk, tɪk
    6. reyn   6. bake a cake   6. leyd, lɪd
    7. leyd
    8. weyt
    9. peynt
   10. pleyz

D. 1. /ɛ—, ɛ—, ɛ—/

2.   (a)   (b)   (c)
    1. stɛp   1. send them   1. bɛd, bæd
    2. tɛn   2. her best dress   2. mɛn, mæn
    3. lɛg   3. a red head   3. lɛt, leyt
    4. prɛs   4. several presents   4. rɛst, reyst
    5. nɛkst   5. when I left   5. wɛəl, wɪəl
    6. lɛŋɵ   6. help the men   6. pɛk, pɪk
    7. frɛš
    8. ɛg
    9. ɛnd
   10. ɛdž

E. 1. /æ—, æ—, æ—/

2.   (a)   (b)   (c)
    1. bæk   1. narrow path   1. bænd, bɛnd
    2. bæŋk   2. past master   2. last, lɛst
    3. fæst   3. half a glass   3. sæd, sɛd
    4. glæd   4. a happy fancy   4. æd, ɛd
    5. pæs   5. a grand family   5. hæt, hat
    6. plænt   6. a black cat   6. sæk, sak
    7. ræg
    8. æz
    9. æsk
   10. ækt

F. It is suggested that five steps be carried out in doing each of the two parts of the following drill: (1) be sure that the students understand the meaning of all the words; (2) let the teacher read across the columns, and the students imitate him; (3) have the students read collectively and individually across the columns; (4) let the teacher dictate ten words selected at random from the drill, and the students write down the words they hear; (5) let the students pick out certain words and try to pronounce them so well that the teacher can recognize them.

1.

	iy		ɪ		ɛ
a.	peak	b.	pick	c.	peck
d.	dean	e.	din	f.	den
g.	deed	h.	did	i.	dead
j.	least	k.	list	l.	lest
m.	heed	n.	hid	o.	head
p.	feel	q.	fill	r.	fell

2.

	ey		ɛ		æ
a.	bait	b.	bet	c.	bat
d.	pain	e.	pen	f.	pan
g.	bake	h.	beck	i.	back
j.	laid	k.	led	l.	lad
m.	lace	n.	less	o.	lass
p.	shale	q.	shell	r.	shall

G. Many of the following sound combinations do not make up English words. First, pronounce them in imitation of your instructor. Then, he will dictate twenty or more combinations chosen from the list at random, while you try to copy down in symbols the sounds he makes.

1.	šiy	11.	riym	21.	fiyt
2.	šɪ	12.	rɪm	22.	fɪt
3.	šey	13.	reym	23.	feyt
4.	šɛ	14.	rɛm	24.	fɛt
5.	šæ	15.	ræm	25.	fæt
6.	šiyp	16.	liyv	26.	siyg
7.	šɪp	17.	lɪv	27.	sɪg
8.	šeyp	18.	leyv	28.	seyg
9.	šɛp	19.	lɛv	29.	sɛg
10.	šæp	20.	læv	30.	sæg

H. Before reading each sentence below, pronounce the two words in parentheses in contrast. Then read each of the sentences twice, using word (a) in the first reading and word (b) in the second. Then read the sentence again using either (a) or (b), while another member of the class tries to identify in each case the word that you pronounced.

1. (a. wean) (b. win) It's time to _____ the child.
2. (a. feel) (b. fill) He doesn't seem to _____ the need.
3. (a. peak) (b. pick) He walked confidently toward the _____.
4. (a. dean) (b. din) I can't study because of the _____.
5. (a. heed) (b. hid) We always _____ our mistakes.
6. (a. sheep) (b. ship) You can't get a _____ into such a small place.
7. (a. bit) (b. bet) I'd like to make a little _____ on that horse.
8. (a. pin) (b. pen) Keep the _____ where you can reach it.
9. (a. pig) (b. peg) I caught the _____ with both hands.
10. (a. rain) (b. wren) The _____ descends gently from the clouds.
11. (a. dale) (b. dell) A great many flowers grow in the _____.
12. (a. laid) (b. led) Who could have _____ the child there?
13. (a. date) (b. debt) I'll never forget that old _____ of mine.
14. (a. mate) (b. mat) The dog was asleep by his _____.
15. (a. cane) (b. can) The cook has a _____ in her hand.
16. (a. mess) (b. mass) In the street was a tangled _____ of cars.
17. (a. pet) (b. pat) It's not wise to _____ a tiger.
18. (a. ten) (b. tan) She's very proud of her _____ shoes.
19. (a. peck) (b. pack) You'll need a whole _____ of cards.
20. (a. shell) (b. shall) You'll shell more peas than I _____.

If the instructor so wishes, the above drill may be used as a test of your ability to distinguish between the front vowel sounds. Take a piece of paper and number the lines from 1 through 20. The instructor will read each sentence, inserting one of the two test words. You should decide which one he used and write (a) or (b) on your paper opposite the number of the sentence.

I.   Read these sentences aloud, making as clear a distinction as possible between the vowels of the words in italics.

1.   Either *read* the book or get *rid* of it.

2.   Didn't you buy *it* to *eat?*

3.   I didn't *seek* to be *sick.*

4.   *Each* foot *itches.*

5.   *List* at *least* the most important ones.

6.   She *dipped deeply* into the sack.

7.   Don't *grin* at my *greenness.*

8.   They *begged* a *big* meal.

9.   There was a sharp noise as the ball *met* his *mitt.*

10. The living influenced us more than the *dead did.*

11. Can you *lift* what's *left?*

12. You'll get *wet* if you *wait.*

13. *Tell* us a *tale*, grandma.

14. There's a *gate* to *get* through.

15. I hope long dresses are a *fading fad.*

16. Bankers *lend* money on *land.*

17. He *said* he was *sad.*

18. His bad *leg* made him *lag* behind.

19. The hen *sat* where he *set* her.

20. You've certainly *met* your *match.*

J.   Read these sentences with two different intonation patterns: (1) so as to create suspense between the two parts of the sentence, and (2) without suspense (see Lesson 6, Section II).

1.   If you do that again, I'll punish you.

2.   You push a little button, and the food comes out.

3.   I opened the door, and there was the "ghost."

4.   When he heard the answer, he was horrified.

5.   If it happens here, it will be the ruin of us.

6.   Until you see me, make no move.

7.   If I'd known that, I could have made ten dollars.

8.   Smoke one of these, and you'll never smoke again.

K. The intonation patterns marked in the selection which follows[1] are somewhat more varied and freer than most of those you have worked with before. Can you control your voice as the lines indicate? This is a good passage for recording.

1. "No, this book is not exactly free, and yet it is free in the sense that you won't actually be paying for it. 2. What you will be paying for is a three-year subscription to Good Homes magazine. 3. And you'll be paying the exact price you'd pay if you went to your local dealer.

4. But by taking a subscription now from me, you also will receive this book of five hundred tested recipes. 5. So, you see, in a manner of speaking, this book is absolutely free. 6. And what's more, madam, you're permitted to take it now, look it over, and return it to me if you decide you don't care to take a subscription to Good Homes magazine."

7. He smiled triumphantly at her. 8. "Could anything be fairer than that?"

L. Read aloud several pages of English, concentrating your attention on the correct formation of the front vowel with which you seem to have most difficulty.

---

[1]Adapted from the story "Profession: Housewife," by Sally Benson, originally published in the *New Yorker*.

Central and Back Vowels

I. The Vowel /a/ as in p<u>o</u>t

You have no doubt noticed that when you visit a physician and he wishes to have a clear view into your mouth and throat, he asks you to say "Ah." That is, of course, the sound of our vowel /a/. The physician knows that the formation of /a/ requires the mouth to be opened more widely than for any other sound. The tongue is also positioned lower in the mouth than for any other vowel. That is what gives the doctor his unobstructed view of your throat.

It might be well here to refer to the vowel chart in Lesson 2 (Figure 3).

In order to form /a/, *the jaw is lowered more than it would be in a normal relaxed position, lowered so far as to require a slight muscular effort. As a consequence, the lips are also wide open, about an inch apart for most speakers,* and two upper front teeth and several lower teeth are probably visible. Verify this with your mirror. *The tongue tip lightly touches a point as low on the floor of the mouth as it can reach, so low that in compensation the back of the tongue must be raised just a little in the throat.*

In most varieties of American English, /a/ is the vowel of *father* /fáðər/, *box* /baks/, and *calm* /kam/. It is most often confused with /ə/ and /æ/. What are the essential differences in the formation of /æ/ and /a/? Check your answer with the description of /æ/ in Lesson 10 and by watching the formation of the two vowels in your mirror.

II. /ɔ/ **as in** b<u>ou</u>ght

In moving from /a/ to /ɔ/, we are starting up the back portion of the vowel chart. The most important thing to watch with this vowel is the position of your lips. The value of a front vowel—/iy/, /ɪ/, /ey/, /ɛ/, or /æ/—is largely determined by the tongue; that is, by the shape and size of the air-escape passage between the tongue and the roof of the mouth. On the other hand, it is the lips—the size and shape of the opening between them—that have most influence in forming the central and back vowels. For /a/ this opening is about an inch and a half across, one inch from top to bottom, and shaped as in Figure 9.

Figure 9. Lip position for /a/

For /ɔ/ the opening is usually about one inch or less across, and half an inch from top to bottom. The lips are somewhat protruded (*pushed forward*). Normally little is to be seen of the teeth. (See Figure 10.) In order for the lips to assume this position for /ɔ/, *the*

Figure 10. Lip position for /ɔ/

jaw is raised a little. The tongue remains in approximately the same position as for /a/, but it is "bunched" a little more toward the back of the mouth.

The /ɔ/-sound is the vowel of *all* /ɔl/, *saw* /sɔ/, *cause* /kɔz/, and *cross* /krɔs/. It is easily confused with /ow/ and /ə/.

III. /ow/ as in b<u>oa</u>t

In order to produce an /ow/, *the lips form the shape of the letter o.* *This requires that they be protruded and rounded more than for /ɔ/.* *The resulting opening is a little circle about half an inch in diameter.* (See Figure 11.) *The jaw has been raised still more, and the "bunching"*

Figure 11. Lip position for /ow/

of the tongue in the back of the mouth is greater. The tongue tip probably no longer touches the floor of the mouth.

Like /ey/, the /ow/-sound is *diphthongized*, much more so in British than in American English. This means that during the pronunciation of the sound the lips close slightly and lose their forced rounding, and the back of the tongue moves upward and backward. The sound is, therefore, symbolized as a vowel plus a glide: /ow/.

The /ow/-sound is the vowel found in *go* /gow/, *cold* /kowld/, *coast* /kowst/, *soul* /sowl/, and *snow* /snow/. It is sometimes confused with /ɔ/ and /uw/. What are the essential differences between /ow/ and /ɔ/? Can you see them with your hand mirror?

IV. /ʊ/ as in p<u>u</u>t

Until now, in order to make the classification of vowels as simple as possible, we have assumed that the progression from /ow/ through /ʊ/ to /uw/ was perfectly regular: that as we moved from one vowel to another up the back part of the vowel chart we merely raised the jaw, rounded the lips, and pulled the tongue backward a little more each time. Actually, the relationship between the back vowels is more complex; the regular progression will account for /ɔ/, /ow/, and /uw/, but not altogether for /ʊ/.

To form /ʊ/, the lips are less rounded and protruded than in the *production of /ow/. The opening between them is wider across than for* */ow/, but a good bit smaller in distance from upper to lower lip.* The teeth may be visible: *the tips of the lower teeth approach the backs of the* *upper ones.* (See Figure 12.) *Though the tongue tip touches nothing,* *the tongue itself is pulled back and up, more than for /ow/, until its* *sides touch the upper tooth ridge.*

Figure 12. Lip position for / ʊ /

The /ʊ/-sound is the vowel of *book* /bʊk/, *full* /fʊl/, and *could* /kʊd/. It is most often confused with /uw/ and /ə/.

V. /uw/ as in bo̲o̲t

Like /iy/, the /uw/-sound requires tension and effort for its production. It is pronounced with a slight upward and backward movement of the tongue after the sound is begun. It is, therefore, symbolized as a vowel plus a glide: /uw/. This diphthongization, however, is much less discernible than in the /ow/-sound. *The lips should be rounded and protruded as much as possible, leaving a little circular opening about the size of a pencil.* The teeth are not visible. (See Figure 13.) *The tip of the tongue is drawn quite far back and*

Figure 13. Lip position for /uw/

touches nothing, but the sides of the tongue press firmly for some distance along the upper tooth ridge.

The /uw/-sound is the vowel of *too* /tuw/, *soon* /suwn/, and *blue* /bluw/. It is easily confused with /ʊ/. Form the two sounds carefully before your hand mirror until you can see and feel clearly the essential difference: (1) in the rounding and protrusion of the lips; (2) in the pressure exerted by the tongue; and (3) in the position of the teeth.

This would be an excellent place, in fact, to review the series of vowels discussed in this lesson—/a-ɔ-ow-ʊ-uw/—and fix in your mind the distinguishing characteristics of the formation of each vowel.

VI. /ə/ as in bu̲t, and /ər/ as in bi̲r̲d.

The only remaining vowel sound is the central, neutral, relaxed /ə/. It has already been described at some length in Lessons 2 and 3 in connection with its very frequent use in unstressed syllables. However, it may be well to add a few more details, by way of comparison, now that you have a clearer understanding of the physiology of the other vowel sounds.

The /ə/-sound *is formed with the lips slightly parted almost their entire length.* (See Figure 14.) *There is no tension or effort anywhere.*

Figure 14. Lip position for /ə/

The tongue lies relaxed on the floor of the mouth, and usually neither its sides nor its tip touches anything.

It is the vowel of *cut* /kət/, *jump* /džəmp/, and *dull* /dəl/. Owing to its position in the center of the vowel chart, it may be confused with any óf the other vowels, though this seems to happen most often with /a/, /ɔ/, and /ʊ/. To change an /ə/ to /a/, open your mouth wide. To change /ə/ to /ʊ/, narrow the lip opening by putting some pressure on the corners of the mouth, touch the sides of the tongue against the upper tooth ridge, and move the teeth closer together.

The combination /ər/ is a complex sound, which, since it includes the glide /r/, is characterized by movement rather than by a fixed position of the speech organs. Though many regional variations of the sound occur, the student from abroad may safely pronounce /ər/ as the symbols indicate—begin it as an ordinary /ə/ and end it as an /r/. *But very little pure /ə/ is heard; even as the /ə/ is formed, it begins to change into an /r/, moving toward the back of the mouth with the sides of the tongue sliding along the tooth ridge and with the tongue tip curving upward without touching anything.* Practice this with *word* /wərd/, *verb* /vərb/, and *turn* /tərn/.

VII. Exercises

A. 1. Listen carefully to your instructor as he pronounces a prolonged /a/ several times: /a—, a—, a—/. Imitate his pronunciation of the vowel, watching your lips, tongue, teeth, etc., in a hand mirror and trying to make your speech organs assume the exact position described in the appropriate section of this lesson.

2. Listen, then imitate, as your instructor pronounces the following material. Finally, try to pronounce each word or phrase to his satisfaction. If he finds that the vowel in a word does not sound

quite right, correct yourself by making your speech organs assume more exactly the desired position.

(a)	(b)	(c)
1. ad	1. start shopping	1. hat, hət
2. aks	2. a garden party	2. stak, stək
3. arm	3. a hot-rod car	3. kap, kəp
4. drap	4. lock the shop	4. nat, nɔt
5. gad	5. stop the clock	5. rak, ræk
6. klak	6. from top to bottom	6. lak, læk
7. lat		
8. martš		
9. gard		
10. dark		

B. The instructions for Exercise A apply also to Exercises B, C, D, E, F, and G.

1. /ɔ—, ɔ—, ɔ—/

2.

(a)	(b)	(c)
1. sɔ	1. tall corn	1. lɔ, low
2. pɔ	2. small talk	2. bɔl, bowl
3. drɔ	3. across the walk	3. kɔst, kowst
4. ɔl	4. a horse's stall	4. strɔŋ, strɔŋ
5. ɔf	5. a soft cloth	5. nɔrs, nərs
6. krɔs	6. along the wall	6. tɔk, tək
7. lɔ		
8. sɔlt		
9. kɔld		
10. bɔrn		

C. 1. /ow—, ow—, ow—/

2.

(a)	(b)	(c)
1. now	1. both soldiers	1. flow, flɔ
2. ðow	2. an open coat	2. kowt, kɔt
3. Θrow	3. those snows	3. nowz, nɔz
4. owld	4. wrote a note	4. kowl, kuwl
5. owd	5. his own show	5. rowz, ruwz
6. bown	6. knows the road	6. powl, puwl
7. smowk		
8. powst		
9. nowt		
10. howps		

D. 1. /ʊ—, ʊ—, ʊ—/

2.   (a)   (b)   (c)

    1. fʊt   1. a good book   1. fʊl, fuwl
    2. pʊl   2. she could cook   2. šʊd, šuwd
    3. tʊk   3. put in sugar   3. wʊd, wuwd
    4. hʊd   4. stood by a brook   4. pʊt, pət
    5. nʊk   5. look at the woman   5. tʊk, tək
    6. šʊr   6. took a book   6. lʊk, lək
    7. pʊš
    8. bʊš
    9. wʊl
   10. wʊlf

E. 1. /uw—, uw—, uw—/

2.   (a)   (b)   (c)

    1. truw   1. a loose tooth   1. šuwt, šət
    2. huw   2. through the school   2. suwn, sən
    3. gluw   3. whose shoe   3. luwk, lʊk
    4. fuwd   4. a blue moon   4. spuwk, spowk
    5. spuwl   5. choose the view   5. tšuwz, tšowz
    6. fruwt   6. move into the room   6. tuwn, town
    7. luwz
    8. pruwv
    9. truwθ
   10. guws

F. 1. /ə—, ə—, ə—/

2.   (a)   (b)   (c)

    1. əp   1. mother tongue   1. šət, šat
    2. əs   2. trouble with bugs   2. klək, klak
    3. həm   3. young love   3. kəm, kam
    4. hənt   4. ugly duckling   4. kət, kɔt
    5. ləŋ   5. wonderful company   5. nən, nuwn
    6. kəp   6. above the cut   6. lək, lʊk
    7. dəst
    8. wəns
    9. rəb
   10. brəš

G. 1. /ər—, ər—, ər—/

2.

	(a)		(b)		(c)
1.	ərθ	1.	the girl's birth	1.	wərm, wɔrm
2.	ərdž	2.	early bird	2.	wərd, wɔrd
3.	fər	3.	a thirsty herd	3.	stər, stɪər
4.	sər	4.	the curves merge	4.	wər, wɛər
5.	stərn	5.	her earnings	5.	bərn, barn
6.	θərd	6.	stern words	6.	lərk, lark
7.	hərt				
8.	wərθ				
9.	bərst				
10.	ərb				

H. Did you ever try to read lips as the deaf must learn to do in order to understand what is said to them? The back vowels and certain consonants are rather easy to recognize by sight. Before doing the following exercise, it would be well to review the pictures of the lip position for central and back vowels and reread, if necessary, the material in Lesson 7 on the point of articulation of /f/ and /p/. Watch in your hand mirror as you form the sounds. In class your instructor will form some of the combinations below with his lips, tongue, etc., without actually uttering any sound. Try to recognize each combination and write down its number.

1.	a	7.	fa	13.	pa
2.	ɔ	8.	fɔ	14.	pɔ
3.	ow	9.	fow	15.	pow
4.	ʊ	10.	fʊ	16.	pʊ
5.	uw	11.	fuw	17.	puw
6.	ə	12.	fə	18.	pə

I. The drills below are to be carried out like Exercise F of the preceding lesson: (1) the teacher makes sure that the meaning of all words is understood; (2) he reads across the columns and the class imitates his pronunciation; (3) the students read across the columns as a group and individually; (4) the teacher dictates ten or more words selected at random; (5) the students pick out certain words and try to pronounce them so well that the teacher can identify them by letter.

1.

	a		ə (and /ər/)		ɔ
a.	not	b.	nut	c.	naught
d.	cod	e.	cud	f.	cawed
g.	Don	h.	done	i.	dawn
j.	cot	k.	cut	l.	caught
m.	are	n.	err	o.	or
p.	barn	q.	burn	r.	born

2.		ɔ		ow		uw
	a.	flaw	b.	flow	c.	flew
	d.	Shaw	e.	show	f.	shoe
	g.	bought	h.	boat	i.	boot
	j.	call	k.	coal	l.	cool
	m.	Paul	n.	pole	o.	pool
	p.	lawn	q.	loan	r.	loon
3.		ə		ʊ		uw
	a.	luck	b.	look	c.	Luke
	d.	cud	e.	could	f.	cooed
	g.	buck	h.	book	i.	
	j.		k.	should	l.	shoed
	m.	putt	n.	put	o.	
	p.		q.	pull	r.	pool

J. Before reading each sentence below, pronounce the two words in parentheses in contrast. Then read each of the sentences below twice, using word (a) in the first reading and word (b) in the second. Then read again and use either (a) or (b), while another member of the class tries to identify in each case the word that you pronounced. The teacher may also give the drill as a test of your ability to distinguish between back vowels.

1. (a. cat) (b. cot)   Would you call it a _____?

2. (a. shack) (b. shock)   He had a _____ in the woods.

3. (a. map) (b. mop)   The _____ was hanging on the wall.

4. (a. far) (b. fur)   Is it _____ from the zoo?

5. (a. doll) (b. dull)   She's wearing a _____ hat.

6. (a. bomb) (b. bum)   One _____ can cause a lot of damage.

7. (a. lock) (b. luck)   We depend on our _____ to avoid burglars.

8. (a. barn) (b. burn)   Take good care of that _____.

9. (a. hall) (b. whole)   Shall we paint the _____ floor?

10. (a. naught) (b. note)   I wrote a _____ on the slip of paper.

11. (a. cost) (b. coast)   The _____ is high along the shore.

12. (a. faun) (b. phone)   Do you have a _____ in your study?

13. (a. awed) (b. owed)   The speaker _____ every man there.

14. (a. horse) (b. hearse)   The _____ was followed by a line of cars.

15. (a. balks) (b. bucks) The pony _____ badly.

16. (a. boat) (b. boot) I'm sure such a _____ will float.

17. (a. foal) (b. fool) She loves that _____ dearly.

18. (a. took) (b. tuck) I _____ the money in my pocket.

19. (a. pull) (b. pool) To have no _____ is a misfortune in Hollywood.

20. (a. school) (b. skull) A _____ can teach many lessons.

If facilities are available, it should be most instructive to record the above drill. You might make notes of the word you intend to use in each sentence: 1-a, 2-b, 3-b, etc. Then record, following your notes, and put the latter away where you cannot see them for several days. After an interval long enough to allow yourself to forget which word you used in each sentence, listen to the recording and write down what you hear. Finally, compare your original notes with the record of what you later heard. You might also have another student listen to your record and make notes of what he hears. Did you in every case hear the word you originally intended to use? Did the other student always hear the same word you heard? Are you now making the central and back vowels with enough clarity to be understood regularly?

K. Read these sentences aloud, making as clear a distinction as possible between the vowels of the words in italics.

1. A *black* cat *blocked* my way.

2. His story only *adds* to the *oddness* of what happened.

3. You'll be *hot* without a *hat*.

4. The sea is *becoming calm*.

5. It fell *suddenly* on the *sod*.

6. The *ducks* swim under the *dock*.

7. We heard a *shot* and *shut* the door.

8. I think he *heard*, though he's *hard* of hearing.

9. When they *woke*, they took a *walk*.

10. Every man brought his own *bowling ball*.

11. I *saw* her *sew* it.

12. The tiger's *claws closed*.

13. It was a noisy *war* of *words*.

14. All was *done* before *dawn*.

15. I *stole* up behind the *stool*.

16.   The results will be *known* by *noon*.

17.   We made a *rush* for the *bushes*.

18.   The child has *good blood*.

19.   He just *stood* and looked at his *food*.

20.   *Soon* the *sun* will come out.

L.   All the sentences in each of the following groups have the same rhythm and intonation. Sentence stresses are marked. Go through each group several times until you can produce that particular pattern rapidly and smoothly.

1.   a.   The bíll has góne to Cóngress.

     b.   The Sénate's slów to páss it.

     c.   The séssion's néarly óver.

     d.   Deláy would cáuse us tróuble.

     e.   We néed to knów the réason.

2.   a.   Spríng is the prélude to súmmer.

     b.   Whát is the náme of the áctor?

     c.   Róbert is táller than Állen.

     d.   Whén is the lády expécted?

     e.   Whó has the cóurage to trý it?

3.   a.   The inflátion may léad to a depréssion.

     b.   It's a fáshion I réad of in the pápers.

     c.   I can gíve you the ánswer in a mínute.

     d.   I'll repéat the suggéstion as I héard it.

     e.   You can sée in a móment that he néeds it.

4.   a.   When the cát's awáy, the míce will pláy.

     b.   If the príce is ríght, I'll búy the cár.

     c.   Though the níghts are cóld, it's wárm todáy.

     d.   As you súrely knów, it's tíme for lúnch.

     e.   Since he séems surprísed, you'd bétter spéak.

M.   Read aloud several pages of English, concentrating your attention on the correct formation of the central or back vowel with which you have most difficulty.

Consonant Substitutions: Part 1

I. Consonant Substitutions

You should be familiar by now with the idea of vowel substitutions, and will probably understand immediately what is meant by the similar phrase, "consonant substitutions." The latter is, of course, that type of speech error in which an incorrect consonant is used in place of the correct one: the pronunciation of *those* as /dowz/ instead of /ðowz/, of *days* as /deys/ instead of /deyz/.

A very large number of such substitutions involve the replacement of a voiced consonant by its voiceless counterpart, or vice versa. We have already treated this type of error in Lessons 7 and 8. In Lessons 12 and 13, we shall work on several common and troublesome consonant substitutions of other kinds, in which the error is not usually due to incorrect voicing. However, a knowledge of the system of consonant classification and the effect an initial or final position may have on a consonant sound—the material of lessons 7 and 8— is basic in attacking the problem before us.

II. /t/ and /θ/, /d/ and /ð/

The English sounds /θ/ and /ð/ occur in very few of the other important tongues of the modern world. Naturally, most students of English as a second language have trouble with the two consonants and often try to replace them in conversational speech by other, more familiar sounds. The most frequent substitutes for /θ/ and /ð/ seem to be /t/ and /d/, respectively, though /s/ and /z/ are sometimes heard also. If you will check back for a moment and think of the points of articulation of these six sounds, you will note how close together they all are.

The consonants /ð/ and /θ/, of course, make a voiced-voiceless pair. In the formation of both, the tip of the tongue should be thrust out quite a way between the upper and lower teeth. To pronounce a perfect /θ/, simply put your tongue between your teeth and blow. Watch in your hand mirror to see how clearly visible the tongue tip is. For /θ/, both initial and final, the air is forced between the teeth with considerable pressure. In fact, the sound is merely the noise of this air rushing out through its narrow passage. For /ð/, there is much less sound of escaping air, this being largely replaced by vibration of the vocal cords. Practice with *teeth* /tiyθ/ and *teethe* /tiyð/, *thigh* /θay/ and *thy* /ðay/, and make the contrast as clear as possible.

When /t/ is substituted for /θ/, as when a Scandinavian or German pronounces *thing* as /tɪŋ/ in place of /θɪŋ/, it means that the tip of the speaker's tongue has merely touched the upper tooth ridge or the back of the upper teeth instead of being thrust between the teeth. Exactly the same thing happens when /d/ replaces /ð/, as when *the* is pronounced /də/ instead of /ðə/. A little more effort is required to make /θ/ and /ð/ than to make /t/ and /d/, since the tongue must move a little farther to produce them.

When /s/ is substituted for /θ/, or /z/ for /ð/, as when the traditional stage Frenchman pronounces *think* as /sɪŋk/ instead of /θɪŋk/, the speaker is making still less effort than the German who used /t/ or /d/. The Frenchman's tongue tip, in forming /s/ or /z/, merely approaches the tooth ridge or upper teeth.

All substitutions of this type are extremely easy to avoid. One merely has to be sure he inserts the tip of the tongue between the teeth when he says /θ/ or /ð/. /θ/ and /ð/ can be seen as easily as they can be heard, and are among the least difficult sounds for a lip-reader to identify. If you will use your mirror, you can tell the difference between /θ-ð/ and /t-d/ or /s-z/ at a glance.

In spite of the ease with which substitutions of /t/ for /θ/ and of /d/ for /ð/ can be corrected when the speaker makes a conscious effort to form them well, they may continue for years to mark his English as "foreign-sounding" at times when he is concentrating on the thought he wishes to express rather than on the position of his tongue. This kind of error is especially persistent in the short un-stressed words of a sentence, where the tendency is to pronounce with as little effort as possible, and where the student from abroad may even have worked hard training himself to avoid too much clarity. The combinations *of the* and *said that* are good examples. To eliminate incorrect /d/'s when he is unself-consciously using such phrases, the student may need to make a considerable disciplined effort. Drills such as those of this lesson may help, especially Exercises A-3 and B-3, in which attention is fixed on the formation of a good /ð/ or /θ/ at the beginning, then gradually transferred to something else. Final and complete elimination, however, will probably require the reading aloud, with attention concentrated on getting the tongue between the teeth for each th, of passages long enough to ensure the formation of an unbreakable habit.

III. /dž/ and /y/

The substitution of /dž/ for /y/ is most often noted in the speech of students whose mother tongue is Spanish. In Argentina /dž/ (or /ž/) has replaced /y/ altogether in words like *yo* and *suya*. In most of Latin America and in Spain this substitution can be heard in words spoken with emphasis. By way of contrast, Scandinavians who learn English tend to make the opposite substitution; in a word like *jump* they are likely to replace /dž/ by /y/, and pronounce /yəmp instead of /džəmp/. Since the manner in which these two consonant sounds are made in English has not yet been explained in this manual, we shall examine them in some detail.

The /y/-sound is essentially a very short and completely un-stressed sound similar to /ɪ/ occurring before some other vowel sound. It is also a glide, which means that it is formed, not in a fixed position, but as the organs of speech move from one place to another. It is heard in words like *yet* /yɛt/ and *young* /yəŋ/. The tongue assumes the /ɪ/-position: tip touching lightly the back of the lower front teeth, sides touching the upper bicuspids. Then voicing begins as the tongue moves immediately to the next vowel in the word. The /y/-sound cannot be very well pronounced alone or separated from the following vowel. You will also remember that /y/ is used with the vowels /iy/ and /ey/ to symbolize an off-glide after the vowel sound.

On the other hand, /dž/ is classified as an affricate. An affricate is a stop (see Lesson 7, Section II) followed by a slow separation of the organs of speech, which makes the last part of the sound a continuant. As the symbol indicates, /dž/ is a combination of /d/ and /ž/. It is voiced, as are both the sounds of which it is composed. You may remember that the voiceless counterpart of /ž/ is /š/. Both /ž/ and /š/ are normally produced by the sound of air rushing through a long shallow channel between the tongue and the hard palate. At the sides, the channel is closed by contact between the sides of the tongue and the tooth ridge. The lips are somewhat protruded and rounded. For the production of /dž/ the position is similar, except that for a moment at the beginning of the sound, the tongue touches the tooth ridge all around, thus blocking altogether the escape of air. When a little pressure has built up, the tip of the tongue (but not the sides) moves away from the tooth ridge, opening the channel for the outrush of air.

If you compare the descriptions of /dž/ and /y/, you will note that the essential difference is this contact at the beginning of /dž/ between the tongue and the upper tooth ridge. For /y/, no part of the tongue touches the roof of the mouth; only light contacts are made between the tongue tip and lower teeth and between the sides of the tongue and the upper bicuspids. Contrast *jet* /džɛt/ and *yet* /yɛt/, and keep your tongue away from your palate and tooth ridge for /y/.

IV. /š/ and /tš/

For reasons which need not be explained here, there is a tendency to substitute /š/ for /tš/ in certain positions, even on the part of students whose mother tongue has a /tš/-sound. Thus *question* is frequently mispronounced as /kwɛššən/ instead of /kwɛstšən/ by speakers of various nationalities.

Since /š/ and /tš/ are the voiceless counterparts of /ž/ and /dž/, they are naturally formed in much the same way, described above, as these latter consonants. Only, in the production of /š/ and /tš/ there is more sound of the outrush of air to make up for the lack of voicing. When /š/ is substituted for /tš/, it simply means that the brief contact between the tongue tip and upper tooth ridge, necessary for /t/, has been omitted. Compare *sheep* /šiyp/ and *cheap* /tšiyp/, *washer* /wašər/ and *watcher* /watšər/.

V. Exercises

A. 1. Listen carefully as your instructor pronounces a prolonged /θ/ several times: /θ—, θ—, θ—/. Imitate his pronunciation of the consonant, making sure that you thrust the tip of your tongue between your teeth.

2. Listen, then imitate, as your instructor pronounces the following material. Finally, try to pronounce each word or phrase to his satisfaction.

(a)

1. θɔ
2. θæŋk
3. θɛft
4. θɪŋk
5. θərd
6. θrow
7. truwθ
8. mənθ
9. ɔ́θər
10. mɛ́θəd

(b)

1. arithmetic
2. thick and thin
3. a thrilling thing
4. beneath his thumb
5. the fourth of the month
6. through the theatre

(c)

1. θɪk, tɪk
2. θiym, tiym
3. θrɛd, trɛd
4. feyθ, feyt
5. pæθ, pæt
6. nə́θɪŋ, nə́tɪŋ
7. šiyθ, šiy:ð
8. lowθ, low:ð
9. tiyθ, tiy:ð
10. íyθər, íyðər
11. θɪk, sɪk
12. θæŋk, sæŋk
13. θəm, səm
14. mawθ, maws
15. tɛnθ, tɛns

3. After you have an opportunity to look at this exercise to be sure you understand all of the words, repeat this drill as rapidly as you can after your instructor. Do not read from the printed page; just imitate what you hear. Each sentence contains at least one /θ/, but you should *not* concentrate on these sounds. Think only of the meaning of the sentence. The instructor will tell you if you mispronounce a /θ/, and you can try again. The drill is intended to help you begin to make the /θ/-sound well when your attention is directed toward the thought of what you are saying.

a. I'm thirsty.
b. I'm methodical.
c. I'm through with it.
d. I'm quite thrilled.
e. I'm thoroughly satisfied.
f. I'm always faithful.
g. I'm having a birthday.
h. I'm in the bathtub.
i. I'm healthily tanned.
j. I'm almost pathetic.
k. I'm thinking hard.
l. I'm very thankful.
m. I'm third in the class.
n. I'm three years older.
o. I'm a thousand miles from home.
p. I'm not a thief.
q. I'm at the theater.
r. I'm going south.
s. I'm losing my teeth.
t. I'm anything you say.

B. The instructions for Exercise A apply also to this exercise.

1. /ð—, ð—, ð—/

2. (a)   (b)

   1. ðæn   1. father and mother
   2. ðiyz   2. get them together
   3. ðɪs   3. smooth feathers
   4. ðaw   4. either this or that
   5. ðəs   5. the weather
   6. suw:ð   6. then and there
   7. briy:ð
   8. léðər
   9. béyðɪŋ
  10. rǽðər

(c)

1.	ðow, dow	6.	tayð, tayd	11.	riy:ð, riyθ
2.	ðey, dey	7.	lowð, lowd	12.	klowð, klowz
3.	ðɛn, dɛn	8.	ə́ðər, ə́dər	13.	siyð, siyz
4.	ðowz, dowz	9.	wə́rðɪ, wə́rdɪ	14.	sayð, sayz
5.	ðɛər, dɛər	10.	ðay, θay	15.	tiyð, tiyz

3. a. You said that you'd rather not.
  b. You said that you'd answer these letters.
  c. You said that you'd be absent this afternoon.
  d. You said that you'd gather up your things.
  e. You said that you'd give clothing.
  f. You said that you'd change those grades.
  g. You said that you'd investigate further.
  h. You said that you'd speak at the beginning of the hour.
  i. You said that you breathed easily.
  j. You said that it bothered you.
  k. You said that you were smothering.
  l. You said that the reverse was the case.
  m. You said that you wouldn't ask this question.
  n. You said that the water was smooth.
  o. You said that you were younger than that.
  p. You said that you liked the idea.
  q. You said that you loathed the place.
  r. You said that you disliked bathing.
  s. You said that you had them already.
  t. You said that they were fun though difficult.

C. 1. Imitate as your teacher pronounces the syllables /dža/ and /ya/ several times. For /dža/, be sure the tongue touches the tooth ridge; for /ya/, avoid such contact carefully.

   2. The exercise below may be carried out as similar drills done previously: (a) the teacher makes sure that the meaning of all words is understood; (b) he reads down the columns, then across them, and the class imitates his pronunciation; (c) the students read across and down, in a group and individually; (d) the teacher dictates several words selected at random; (e) the students pick out certain words and try to pronounce them so well that the teacher can identify them by letter.

	dž		y
a.	Jew	b.	you
c.	juice	d.	use (noun)
e.	jet	f.	yet
g.	jarred	h.	yard
i.	joke	j.	yoke
k.	jail	l.	Yale

   3. Read these sentences aloud, making as clear a distinction as possible between the /dž/ and /y/ of the italicized words.

     a. He has been *jeered* at for *years*.

     b. You can't make *jam* with *yams*.

     c. *You lie*; it was in *July*.

     d. The oranges are *juiceless* and *useless*.

     e. Please *yell* when the mixture *jells*.

D. The instructions for Exercise C also apply to this exercise.

   1. /šow-tšow, šow-tšow, šow-tšow/

   2.

	š		tš
a.	sheep	b.	cheap
c.	ship	d.	chip
e.	shatter	f.	chatter
g.	mush	h.	much
i.	mashing	j.	matching
k.	washer	l.	watcher

   3. a. The baby shouldn't *chew* his *shoe*.

     b. Merchants try to *catch* all the *cash* they can.

     c. I never *wished* to see such a *witch*.

     d. He uses *crutches* since his foot was *crushed*.

     e. You were *cheated* when you bought that *sheet*.

E. Your instructor will dictate some of the words from the exercise below for you to recognize and write down. Then you should choose certain of them, not in any fixed order, and try to pronounce them well enough so that he can identify them. In the phonetic transcription of each word, marks of length, /ː/, and aspiration, /ʰ/, have been added where appropriate (see Lesson 8), in order to help you pronounce more clearly.

1.	dead	/dɛːd/		11.	heart	/hart/
2.	death	/dɛθ/		12.	hard	/haːrd/
3.	debt	/dɛt/		13.	hearth	/harθ/
4.	thread	/θrɛːd/		14.	tie	/tʰay/
5.	dread	/drɛːd/		15.	die	/day/
6.	tread	/trʰɛːd/		16.	thy	/ðay/
7.	threat	/θrɛt/		17.	thigh	/θay/
8.	sink	/sɪŋk/		18.	sigh	/say/
9.	zinc	/zɪŋk/		19.	breath	/brɛθ/
10.	think	/θɪŋk/		20.	bread	/brɛːd/
				21.	breadth	/brɛːdθ/

F. This exercise is a review of the consonants which have been practiced in this lesson, and it can be used in different ways. (1) Combine the introductory phrases on the left with each item on the right to practice all of the sentences. (2) Your instructor will call out a letter, and you are to make a sentence by combining one of the introductory phrases on the left with the phrase which bears that letter. (3) When your instructor says "think," you are to use only the phrase "He thought that he should . . ." to make sentences, and when your instructor says "wish," you are to use only the phrase "He wished that he could . . ." to make sentences.

a. wash the car

b. thank the teacher

c. watch television

He thought that he should . . .   d. use the telephone

e. go to the theatre

f. joke about the matter

He wished that he could . . .   g. shut the door

h. breathe deeply

i. tell the truth

j. choose something else

G. This exercise is to be carried out like exercises done earlier.

1. (a. thought) (b. taught)   I would never have _____ that.

2. (a. booth) (b. boot)   That _____ is too small.

3. (a. thinking) (b. sinking)   Are you _____ or just lying
there?

4. (a. truth) (b. truce)   We must have the _____ at all costs.

5. (a. They've) (b. Dave)   _____ sat there for hours without
moving.

6. (a. these) (b. d's)   Can you pronounce _____ perfectly?

7. (a. soothe) (b. sued)   He declared he'd _____ her.

8. (a. teething) (b. teasing)   I believe the child is only _____.

9. (a. jail) (b. Yale)   My son just got out of _____.

10. (a. jet) (b. yet)   The color is not _____ black.

11. (a. joke) (b. yolk)   I see no _____ in that egg.

12. (a. jeers) (b. cheers)   Don't let their _____ disturb you.

13. (a. shin) (b. chin)   He hit me on the _____.

14. (a. share) (b. chair)   Don't take my _____ from me.

15. (a. dish) (b. ditch)   Put the ashes in the _____.

16. (a. washing) (b. watching)   What are you _____ so carefully?

H. The sentences in each of the following groups have the same rhythm and
intonation. Repeat each group until you can produce that particular
pattern rapidly and smoothly.

1. a. Can you ánswer it for me?
    b. Won't you téll us about it?
    c. Is he shówing it to them?
    d. You're antágonizing him?
    e. You presénted me to her?

2. a. Tóm is a gréat bíg bóy.
    b. Whích is the síxtéenth flóor?
    c. Thís is a óne-mán shów.
    d. Whát was in lást níght's néws?
    e. Whó has the bést báss vóice?

3. a. It's a lóng tíme since I have séen you.

 b. It's a góod thíng that he's an áthlete.

 c. There's a réal réason for precáutions.

 d. It's a lóng wáy to San Francísco.

 e. She was quíte háppy to be chósen.

4. a. It's nót wíse to téll them what you léarned.

 b. There's nó wáy to bríng it to the shóre.

 c. A níce cúp of cóffee would be góod.

 d. A lóud "nó" was áll that he could sáy.

 e. My óld shóes are pléasant to put ón.

If facilities are available, the above drill may be recorded.

I. Read aloud several pages of English, concentrating your attention on avoiding whichever of the consonant substitutions treated in this lesson you have noticed in your own speech.

Consonant Substitutions: Part 2

I. /b/, /v/, /w/, and /hw/

These four sounds—/b/, /v/, /w/, and /hw/—form a group within which are made several different substitutions not due to incorrect voicing. Students whose original tongue was Spanish or Tagalog tend to confuse /b/ and /v/, because of the lack of a clear distinction between the two consonants in those languages; it may seem to an American ear that such students pronounce *visit* as /bɪzɪt/ instead of /vɪzɪt/. Scandinavians, Central Europeans, Iranians, members of the Arabic-speaking group, and some others often substitute /v/ for /w/, give *we* the improper sound of /viy/ in place of /wiy/. Latin Americans may prefix a /g/ to words which begin with /w/; *would* /wʊd/ thus becomes /gwʊd/. Since /hw/ does not exist in many languages, there is a rather general tendency to replace it in English by /w/; *where* /hwɛər/ becomes /wɛər/, *white* /hwayt/ becomes /wayt/.

These substitutions are easily made because all four of the sounds—/b/, /v/, /w/, and /hw/—are produced far forward in the mouth, largely with the lips, the teeth, and the tip of the tongue.

You may remember that /b/ is a voiced stop, made between the lips. For an initial or medial /b/, the lips close firmly, the pressure of air trying to escape builds up briefly behind them, and then the air is released by a sudden opening of the lips: try it with *berry* /b̠ɛɪ/. In the production of a final /b/, the last part of the process, the explosive release of the air as the lips open, is usually not heard (see Lesson 8, Section III). Can you pronounce *rob* /rab/, and allow the sound to end while your lips are still closed?

By way of contrast, /v/ is a voiced continuant, made between upper *teeth* and lower lip. The cutting edge of the upper teeth touches lightly the lower lip, and the air escapes smoothly, without being stopped even momentarily. It should be clear, then, that all that is necessary in order to avoid the substitution of /b/ for /v/ is to touch the lower lip against the *teeth* rather than against the *upper lip*. *Very, berry;* /v̠ɛɪ/, /b̠ɛɪ/; light touch against upper teeth, firm closure of lips.

The /w/-sound is a glide, as is /y/. Essentially, /w/ is a very short and unstressed /u/, from which the speaker passes immediately to some full vowel sound. It is heard in words like *went* /w̠ɛnt/, and *once* /w̠əns/. The glide begins with the lips protruded and rounded in the /u/-position (see Lesson 11, Section V); from there the speech organs move on quickly to the position for the following vowel, whatever it may be. You will also remember that /w/ is the symbol used with the vowels /ow/, /uw/, and /aw/ to show an upward glide. In avoiding the substitution of /v/ for /w/, it is most important to protrude the lips and keep the lower lip away from the upper teeth. If this lip even brushes the teeth, the /w/ will have some of the /v/-quality about it and may be misunderstood. Contrast *wine* /w̠ayn/ and *vine* /v̠ayn/, *west* /w̠ɛst/ and *vest* /v̠ɛst/.

The remaining sound in this group, /hw/, is also a glide. It is sometimes known as the "candle-blowing sound," because we make it by emitting a little puff of air through the rounded and protruded lips, just as we do when we want to blow out a candle or match. No such puff of air accompanies the formation of /w/. You can see the difference between these two sounds if you will hold a lighted match about two inches from your lips as you pronounce *witch* /w̠ɪtš/ and *which* /hw̠ɪtš/. *Witch* should hardly cause the flame to flicker, but a properly produced *which* should blow it out.

It should be pointed out that the substitution of /w/ for /hw/ cannot always be regarded as an error. Good American speakers often make it, especially when pronouncing rapidly such words as *which, where, what, why,* and *when* in unstressed positions. In some forms of British English, /w/ for /hw/ is common even in stressed words like *whale* and *white*. Such substitutions can sometimes result in misunderstanding, however, and it is certainly worthwhile for the student of American English to understand that there can be a difference in the pronunciation of such words.

II. Final /n/, /ŋ/, and /ŋk/

At the end of words, there is often confusion between /n/, /ŋ/, and /ŋk/. Some Chinese and Latin American students are accustomed to pronouncing all final n̲'s as /ŋ/ in their own language, and find it quite hard not to carry the habit over into English. In their mouths *rain* /reyn̲/ becomes /reyŋ/, and *seen* /siyn̲/ sounds like /siyŋ/. On the other hand, there is another group, especially those whose mother tongue is German or certain of the Central European languages, who often add a /k/ to words which should end with an /ŋ/-sound; they pronounce *doing* /dúwɪŋ/ as /dúwɪŋk/.

The consonants /n/ and /ŋ/, along with /m/, form the group known as nasals, a classification which we have not so far discussed. In the production of other consonants (orals) the air escapes through the mouth; for the nasals it comes out through the nose. It is the soft palate, or velum, which determines which way the air shall escape. When the velum is drawn up, it closes the nasal passage and forces the air out through the mouth. When the velum is relaxed, the breath stream may pass out either through mouth or nose. To produce a nasal consonant, the velum is relaxed and at the same time the passage through the mouth is blocked at some point by the tongue or lips, so that all the air is forced out through the nose. All normal nasals are voiced. The diagrams in Figure 15 should help you visualize the essential differences between an oral consonant and the nasals /m/, /n/, and /ŋ/.

It will be seen that for /m/ the outflow of air through the mouth is blocked by the closing of the lips, for /n/ it is blocked by the tongue's touching the tooth ridge, and for /ŋ/ by the tongue's bunching in the back of the mouth and pressing against the palate.

To avoid the substitution of /ŋ/ for /n/, then, it is only necessary to see that the back of the tongue is low and that the tongue tip and blade touch the tooth ridge all around with sufficient firmness to block the escape of air through the mouth. Note the clear contrast in tongue positions for *ran* /ræn̲/ and *rang* /ræŋ/, *sin* /sɪn̲/ and *sing* /sɪŋ/.

The substitution of /ŋk/ for /ŋ/ is a little more difficult to control. One of the causes for it is probably a feeling on the part of the speaker that the final g̲ of a word like *doing* should be pronounced.

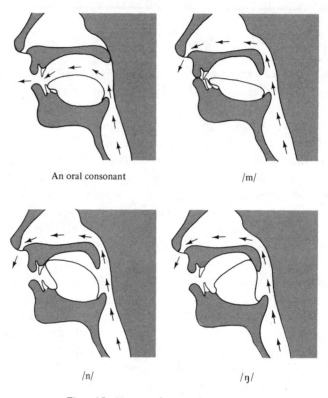

An oral consonant   /m/

/n/   /ŋ/

Figure 15. Air escape for an oral consonant and
the nasal consonants

Since /g/ is a voiced sound, a person in whose native language final
voiced consonants are not common will tend to substitute for /g/
its voiceless counterpart, /k/. It should be understood clearly that
the g of the ending -ng is silent; the g changes the preceding n from
/n/ to /ŋ/, but it is not itself pronounced. You may be able to
realize this fact better if you will note the contrasting pronunciations
of *singer* and *finger*. The former is /sĭŋər/; the g is silent, though it
affects the sound of n. The latter is /fĭŋgər/; the g not only changes
the n, but is also pronounced itself. Can you hear the difference
between /ŋ/ and /ŋg/? At the end of a word -ng always has the
sound of /ŋ/, as in *singer*.

You may have noticed that /ŋ/, /g/, and /k/ are all formed
with the tongue in the same position, bunched high in the back of

the mouth so as to touch the palate. Two of these, /g/ and /k/, are oral stops. To produce them, the velum is drawn up, preventing the escape of air through the nose. The tongue momentarily blocks the passage of air through the mouth, then releases it explosively. The other, /ŋ/, is a nasal continuant. The velum is relaxed, allowing the air to pass out through the nose. The tongue, which blocks the passage through the mouth, remains in its position until the end of the sound. There is no explosive release of breath. The substitution of /ŋk/ for /ŋ/ may be avoided, then, by taking care that there shall be no explosive release, no aspiration, at the end of a word like *rang*. The tongue should remain pressed against the palate until the sound is completely finished. Contrast *rang* /ræŋ̱/ and *rank* /ræŋ̱k/, *sing* /sɪŋ̱/ and *sink* /sɪŋ̱k/.

III. /h/

The problem with /h/ is not usually substitution, but omission. It is another of those English sounds which do not occur in certain other languages, notably French, Italian, and Portuguese. In Spanish the /h/-sound exists, but is given to the letter j; the letter h is always silent. This means that speakers of one of the Latin languages may have difficulty in producing /h/, and find it natural simply to ignore the sound.

This tendency is probably strengthened by the fact that in a few common English words the h really should be left silent: *heir* /ɛər/, *honor* /ánər/, and *hour* /awr/. Either pronunciation, with or without /h/ is possible for *herb*, /ərb/ or /hərb/; *homage* /hámɪdž/ or /ámɪdž/; and *humble*, /həmbəl/ or /əmbəl/. Furthermore, native speakers of English frequently omit the /h/ of little words such as *he, him, his, her, have, has,* and *had, when these are in an unstressed position* in the sentence: *Tell him now* /tɛ́əl ɪm náw/; *We have done it* /wiy əv dən ɪt/.

Except in the cases mentioned above, all initial h's should be sounded. Even with *he, him*, etc., it is certainly not necessary to omit the h in order to avoid a "foreign accent."

The /h/-sound is a voiceless continuant, and no particular position of the tongue and lips is required to produce it. With the speech organs in the position of the sound which is to follow /h/, the breath is forced through the partially closed vocal cords and out of the mouth with sufficient strength to make a rushing sound (as if the speaker were panting for breath): *home* /ẖowm/, *house* /ẖaws/.

IV. Exercises

A. 1. Listen carefully as your instructor pronounces a prolonged /v/ several times: /v—, v—, v—/. Imitate his pronunciation making sure that the cutting edge of your upper teeth touches your lower lip.

   2. Listen, then imitate, as your instructor pronounces the following material. Finally try to pronounce each word or phrase to his satisfaction.

   a.
1. veyn	6. vízıt	11. ınvéyd
2. vɛst	7. vílıdž	12. ınváyt
3. vɔys	8. ləv	13. kə́vər
4. vyuw	9. breyv	14. əlέvən
5. hέvı	10. sέvən	15. peyvd

   b.
1. various vegetables	7. a vivid blue
2. overly virtuous	8. a very bad verdict
3. never vexed	9. an oval table
4. verify the victory	10. a back vowel
5. a vicious savage	11. a bold visitor
6. a big vote	12. a beautiful valley

   c.
1. veyn, weyn	6. vowt, bowt
2. vɛst, wɛst	7. vέrı, bέrı
3. vέrı, wέrı	8. kə́ver, kə́bərd
4. vɛks, wæks	9. rówvıŋ, rówbıŋ
5. veys, weyst	10. veyn, beyn

   3. After you have an opportunity to look at this exercise to be sure you understand all of the words, repeat this drill as rapidly as you can after your instructor. Concentrate on the *thought* of the sentences, and depend upon your instructor to call to your attention any /v/ that is mispronounced.

   a. I've sealed the envelope.
   b. I've had very little vacation.
   c. I've prevented an accident.
   d. I've never tried to write verse.
   e. I've read Volume I.
   f. I've just left my favorite class.
   g. I've several vices.
   h. I've spilled gravy on my vest.
   i. I've never even seen it.
   j. I've lost some valuable papers.
   k. I've never driven a Cadillac.
   l. I've learned all vowels are voiced.

B. 1. Imitate as your teacher pronounces /wiy/, /wiy/, /wiy/; /wow/, /wow/, /wow/. Be sure your lips are rounded and protruded, and that you keep your lower lip away from your teeth as you pronounce /w/.

2. a. 1. wey
        2. wɔl
        3. wɛnt
        4. wər
        5. kwɪk

        6. kwáyət
        7. swɪm
        8. ɔ́lweyz
        9. bɪwɛ́ər
        10. bɪtwíyn

        11. weyt
        12. əwéyt
        13. kwɛ́stšən
        14. wɛ́stərn
        15. wúmən

    b. 1. within a week
        2. gone with the wind
        3. wish me well
        4. waste away
        5. awaken at once
        6. without vigor

        7. a vast world
        8. a loving wife
        9. vile weather
        10. win over
        11. a wicked villain
        12. the seven wonders of the world

3. After looking at this exercise to be sure you understand all of the words, repeat the drill after your instructor. Concentrate on the *thought* of the sentences, and depend upon your instructor to call your attention to any mispronounced /w/'s.

    a. I wish I were wiser.
    b. I wish I had a sandwich.
    c. I wish I weighed less.
    d. I wish I knew more words.
    e. I wish I could find work.
    f. I wish I were widely read.
    g. I wish we had won.
    h. I wish we were through.
    i. I wish you would warn us.
    j. I wish you would reward us.
    k. I wish the window were open.
    l. I wish to ask a question.

C. 1. With your hand before your lips, pronounce /way/ and /hway/ several times. You should be able to feel the puff of air with which /hway/ is produced.[1]

---

[1]Note to the teacher: Because many varieties of British and American English do not always distinguish /h/ and /hw/, it is unnecessary to spend much time on this distinction, particularly if students have a great deal of trouble with it.

2. a. 1. hwaɪ   5. hwaɪt   9. hwaɪn
        2. hweɪl   6. hwɪp   10. ɛ́vrɪhwɛɚr
        3. hwɛn   7. hwiyl   11. hwɛnɛ́vər
        4. hwɪtš   8. əhwáyl   12. hwiyt

    b. 1. the white whale   7. wash his whiskers
        2. which wharf   8. a wild whistle
        3. the whip whistled   9. whisk away
        4. a whiff of whiskey   10. while the wind whirled
        5. whine and whimper   11. whether we want it or not
        6. wherever you wish   12. when she winked

3. a. I know what you want us to do.
    b. I know what we're to study.
    c. I know what a whirlwind is.
    d. I know what you whispered.
    e. I know nowhere to look.
    f. I know where the laboratory is.
    g. I know when we make recordings.
    h. I know when I pronounce it right.
    i. I know all your whims.
    j. I know which bus to take.
    k. I know why the wheels turn.
    l. I know why we're doing this.

D. 1. Imitate your teacher's pronunciation of /ræn/, /ræŋ/, /ræŋk/
        several times. Be sure that your tongue touches your tooth ridge
        for /n/, your palate for /ŋ/, and that there is no explosive release
        of breath for either sound.

    2. This exercise is to be carried out similarly to previous exercises of
        this kind.

n		ŋ		ŋk	
a.	sin	b.	sing	c.	sink
d.	thin	e.	thing	f.	think
g.	win	h.	wing	i.	wink
j.	son	k.	sung	l.	sunk
m.	bun	n.	bung	o.	bunk
p.	ban	q.	bang	r.	bank

    3. Read these sentences aloud, making as clear a distinction as possible
        between the /n/, /ŋ/, and /ŋk/ of the italicized words.

        a. They *ran* and *rang* the bell.
        b. A new *gang* war *began*.

   c. I think he's *kin* to the *king.*

   d. It's *pinching* my *chin.*

   e. Come *on;* get *along.*

   f. A pilot must *win* his *wings.*

   g. What are you *doing* with the *ink?*

   h. The Titanic's passengers *sang* as the ship *sank.*

   i. Are you *ordering drinks?*

   j. I *think* the *thing* is possible.

   k. The chains *clank* and *clang.*

   l. The flowers are *dropping* their *pink* petals.

E. 1. Imitate your teacher's pronunciation of /huw/, /huw/, /huw/; /hey/, /hey/, /hey/. You should be able to feel the strong puff of air at the beginning of each of these syllables.

   2. a.

1.	haws	6.	howld	11.	pərhǽps
2.	huw	7.	hɔrs	12.	bɪhéyv
3.	how	8.	hiyt	13.	bɪháynd
4.	hɪər	9.	hərt	14.	hə́ŋgrɪ
5.	heyt	10.	əhéd	15.	hǽmbərgər

      b.

1.	hard-hearted	5.	a happy home
2.	high-handed	6.	my only hope
3.	the whole of history	7.	hurricane winds
4.	Uncle Henry	8.	have and hold

   3. After going over this exercise to be sure you understand all of the words, repeat the drill after your instructor. Concentrate on the *thought* of the sentences and depend upon your instructor to call your attention to the omission of any /h/'s which should not be omitted.

     a. I hear you've been in the hospital.

     b. I hear you've heard from home.

     c. I hear you're going away for the holidays.

     d. I hear you know how to manage a horse.

     e. I hear you hope to hire some help.

     f. I hear you've been hesitating to ask for help.

     g. I hear he's been misbehaving.

     h. I hear he always has high grades.

     i. I hear he's not happy here.

     j. I hear he habitually makes errors.

     k. I hear she has a beautiful head of hair.

l. I hear it has already happened.
m. I hear they're holding open house.
n. I hear I must meet the American history requirement.
o. I hear the instructor is hard to please.

F. This exercise is to be carried out like similar exercises done previously.

b	v	w	hw
1. bail	2. veil	3. wail	4. whale
5. buy	6. vie	7. Y	8. why
9. bile	10. vile	11. wile	12. while
13. bet	14. vet	15. wet	16. whet
17.	18. vine	19. wine	20. whine
21. best	22. vest	23. west	24.

G. In order to help fix in your mind the position in which the consonants studied in these last two lessons and the back vowels are formed, another lip-reading exercise is included here. Your instructor will form some of the combinations below with his lips, tongue, etc., without actually uttering any sound. Try to recognize each combination and write down its number.

1. ba	7. wa	13. da
2. bow	8. wow	14. dow
3. bə	9. wə	15. də
4. va	10. ða	16. ša
5. vow	11. ðow	17. šow
6. və	12. ðə	18. šə

H. This exercise is to be carried out like similar exercises previously done.

1. (a. bow) (b. vow)   He made a _____ to greet us cordially.
2. (a. boat) (b. vote)   The candidate received a large _____.
3. (a. bat) (b. vat)   A _____ is used in making beer.
4. (a. veil) (b. wail)   A _____ is a sign of sorrow.
5. (a. verse) (b. worse)   It couldn't possibly be _____.
6. (a. vines) (b. wines)   Californians should know about

_____.

7. (a. way) (b. whey)   Make _____for the dairy truck.
8. (a. wetting) (b. whetting)   Why are you _____ your knife?
9. (a. ton) (b. tongue)   Does it weigh as much as a _____?

10. (a. sin) (b. sing) Don't urge me to _____.
11. (a. stun) (b. stung) Your remarks _____ me.
12. (a. wing) (b. wink) The waitress gave me a _____.
13. (a. sing) (b. sink) The child won't _____ in the water.
14. (a. bang) (b. bank) I wouldn't _____ on the door, if I were you.
15. (a. hitch) (b. itch) I hope no _____ will develop.
16. (a. heart) (b. art) Put your _____ in your work.
17. (a. heating) (b. eating) I won't live there because of the _____ arrangements.

I. This exercise gives you another opportunity to familiarize yourself with natural intonation patterns by making your voice follow a visible line. As you work on the passage,[2] write in such phonetic symbols and markings as you feel would help you with any pronunciation difficulties you may still be having. The material is suitable for recording.

1. The young man took a watch from his pocket and looked at it.

2. "I guess we'd better make it snappy if we're going to the last show,"

he said. 3. "Just about ten minutes is all we've got." 4. "Oh," said

she. 5. "Where shall we go?" he persisted; "is there anything special

you'd like to see? 6. What's on, anyway; have you got a paper?"

7. "There isn't anything special. 8. I guess I've seen just about every-

thing, as a matter of fact." 9. "Me too." 10. She suggested timidly,

---

[2]Adapted from the story "My Sister Frances" by Emily Hahn, originally published in the *New Yorker*.

"Do we have to go to the movies?"   11. "Why, don't you want to?"

12. "If you don't think you'd get tired of me," she murmured, "I'd just as soon we stayed right here like this."

J.   Read aloud several pages of English, concentrating your attention on avoiding whichever of the consonant substitutions treated in this lesson you have noticed in your own speech.

Consonant Clusters

I. Problems with Consonant Clusters

By now you have been introduced to and have practiced all of the consonant sounds of English. Hopefully, you have learned to produce even the ones which are most difficult for you. However, English allows many clusters of consonants—that is, sequences of two or more consonants within a syllable—which are especially troublesome for speakers of languages which do not permit such sequences.

Speakers of Spanish and Persian, for example, find it difficult to produce an initial consonant cluster like /sp-/ without placing a vowel before it. They tend to say /ɛ-spik/ for *speak* or /ɛ-stúwdənt/ for *student*. Speakers of Hindi do much the same thing, except they use a different vowel: /ɪ-spiyk/ and /ɪ-stúwdənt/.

Speakers of other languages resolve the consonant cluster problem in another way. Speakers of Chinese, for example, sometimes say /ka-riym/ for *cream* or /sta-riyt/ for *street*.

More of a problem for many speakers than the initial consonant clusters are those which come in final position. The addition of the -s and -ed endings frequently produce consonant clusters which students find difficult to pronounce: *asks* /æsks/, *watched* /watšt/, *changed* /tšeyndžd/.

Furthermore, even if a student has learned to pronounce individual consonant clusters, he may have difficulty when words with final clusters occur in the stream of speech next to words which begin with initial clusters. These consonant combinations at word borders can become quite complex: *changed three* /—ndžd ər—/, *learned gladly* /—rnd gl—/, *looked strong* /—kt str—/. When, by the coming together of two words, a combination of consonants is produced which is quite hard to pronounce, such as *these three* /ðiyz ᶿriy/ or *first grade* /fərst greyd/, there is a strong tendency for new speakers of English to separate the words and thus make the combination easier by inserting a finishing sound between them. This results in unnatural pronunciations such as /ðiyzə ᶿriy/ and /fərstə greyd/. The transition from /z/ to /θ/ and from /t/ to /g/ must be made quickly and directly so that no finishing sound may creep in.

This lesson will explore ways in which the production of these consonant clusters and consonant combinations can be made less difficult. It will also provide practice of the most frequently occurring consonant clusters, both in individual words and in the stream of speech.

II. Consonant Clusters in Initial Position

Unlike many languages, English permits from one to three consonants at the beginning of a word: *rate* /reyt/, *trait* /trayt/, *straight* /streyt/. The table on page 151 lists all of the consonant clusters which are permitted in initial position in English, with word examples of each.[1]

Not all of the initial consonant clusters occur with equal frequency in English (for example, the /skl-/ of *sclerosis* is extremely infrequent), nor are all initial clusters of equal difficulty. Clusters made up of one or two consonants plus /y/ or /w/ are not usually as troublesome for most speakers as are others.

Initial clusters of consonants plus /r/ or /l/ are of high frequency in English. These are particularly difficult for Oriental students. (See Lesson 9.) Once the production of /r/ and /l/ is learned well, these clusters will no longer be a problem, but care must be exercised to maintain a clear distinction between such words as *pray* and *play* or *fly* and *fry*.

---

[1]The data on consonant clusters in this lesson are taken from Betty Jane Wallace, "A Quantitative Analysis of Consonant Clusters in Present-Day English," Dissertation, University of Michigan, 1951.

TABLE OF INITIAL CONSONANT CLUSTERS

/sp/	spin	/kr/	crow	/pl/	play
/st/	stay	/br/	bring	/kl/	clay
/sk/	sky	/dr/	drink	/bl/	blue
/sf/	sphere	/gr/	grey	/gl/	glue
/sm/	small	/fr/	free	/fl/	flew
/sn/	snail	/Θr/	three	/sl/	slew
/tw/	twin	/šr/	shrink	/spy/	spew
/kw/	quick	/by/	beauty	/sky/	skew
/dw/	dwell	/py/	pure	/skw/	squall
/gw/	Guam	/ky/	cure	/spr/	spray
/sw/	swim	/vy/	view	/str/	stray
/hw/	when	/fy/	few	/skr/	scratch
/Θw/	thwart	/hy/	hue	/spl/	split
/pr/	pray	/my/	mute	/skl/	sclerosis
/tr/	tray				

III. Initial s̲ Followed by a Consonant

A particularly difficult consonant cluster is one which begins with an initial /s/ followed by another consonant (/st-/ *stop*) or by a consonant plus an /r/ or /l/ (/str-/ *string*, /spl-/ *splash*). Students whose mother tongue does not permit such sequences are tempted to precede these clusters with a vowel sound: *state* is pronounced as /ɛsteyt/, *spirit* as /ɛspírɪt/, *scrap* as /ɛskræp/. This type of mispronunciation can usually be avoided by concentrating on the /s/-sound and consciously lengthening it: /s—teyt/, /s—pírɪt/, /s—kræp/.

An error which some students make in pronouncing the /sl-/, /sm-/, /sn-/ clusters is to substitute a /z/-sound for the /s/. In other words, they begin voicing for the /l/, /m/, or /n/ too soon. Thus *smoke* sounds like /z̲mowk/. Again, the way to avoid this is to concentrate on lengthening the /s/-sound without voicing it, and then to pronounce the following consonant very rapidly: /s—mowk/.

IV. Consonant Clusters in Final Position

The English language permits many more consonant clusters in final position than in initial position, but many of these are of very low frequency: /-ŋst/ *amongst* or /-ltst/ *waltzed*. Others occur over and over again in normal conversation. The /-nt/ cluster appeared over 200 times and the /-ts/ over 100 times in 10,000 words—about an hour and a half of recorded speech.

The table below lists all of the consonant clusters which can occur in final position in English, with word examples of each. Notice that many of these are formed because of the addition of the -s or -ed endings. Of the 178 clusters listed, however, it was found that only about 70 are used with regularity in ordinary speech. Furthermore, only about 35 of these 70 occurred five or more times in 10,000 words. In the table below the most frequently used consonant clusters are marked with an asterisk (*). More attention should be paid to these than to the others.

TABLE OF FINAL CONSONANT CLUSTERS

*/lp/	help	/rb/	barb	/dθ/	width
*/lt/	belt	/rg/	berg	/pθ/	depth
/lk/	milk	/rv/	curve	/fθ/	fifth
*/lf/	self	/rm/	arm	/ltš/	filch
*/lθ/	wealth	*/rn/	barn	/ldž/	bulge
/lb/	bulb	*/rs/	farce	/rtš/	march
*/lv/	delve	/rš/	harsh	/rdž/	barge
/lm/	film	*/rl/	girl	/ntš/	pinch
/ln/	kiln	/nθ/	month	*/ndž/	range
*/ls/	else	*/ns/	once	/mpt/	tempt
/lš/	Welsh	/nf/	Banff	/rmθ/	warmth
/sp/	wasp	*/nt/	ant	/ksθ/	sixth
/sk/	ask	/mp/	camp	*/rnt/	burnt
/rp/	harp	/mt/	dreamt	/dst/	midst
*/rt/	heart	/mf/	nymph	/lfθ/	twelfth
*/rk/	hark	*/ŋk/	link	/ŋst/	amongst
/rf/	scarf	/ŋθ/	length	/lft/	delft
*/rθ/	hearth	/tθ/	eighth		
*/pt/	stopped	/bd/	robbed	/bz/	cabs
*/kt/	liked	/gd/	tagged	*/dz/	beds
/ft/	laughed	/vd/	lived	/gz/	tags
/θt/	lathed	/ðd/	bathed	/ðz/	bathes
*/st/	passed	/md/	seemed	*/mz/	seems
*/št/	washed	*/nd/	cleaned	*/nz/	cleans
*/ps/	stops	/ŋd/	longed	*/ŋz/	things
*/ks/	likes	*/ld/	filled	*/lz/	fills
*/ts/	eats	*/rd/	marred	*/rz/	cars
/θs/	baths	*/zd/	caused	/vz/	lives
/fs/	laughs	/žd/	rouged	/lt/	felt

/tšt/	watched	/rft/	surfed	/rθt/	earthed
/džd/	judged	/mft/	triumphed	/lps/	helps
/lpt/	helped	/lst/	repulsed	/rps/	harps
/rpt/	harped	*/rst/	forced	/mps/	camps
/mpt/	camped	/nst/	sensed	/sps/	wasps
/spt/	clasped	/tst/	Ritzed	/lks/	milks
/lkt/	milked	/pst/	lapsed	*/rks/	works
/rkt/	worked	/kst/	taxed	*/ŋks/	links
/ŋkt/	linked	/lšt/	Welshed	/sks/	asks
/skt/	asked	/ršt/	marshed	/lts/	belts
/rts/	hearts	/rfs/	surfs	/dzd/	adzed
/nts/	ants	/mfs/	nymphs	/lbz/	bulbs
/mts/	tempts	/pθs/	depths	/rbz/	barbs
/sts/	tests	/fθs/	fifths	/ldz/	holds
/pts/	crypts	/lbd/	bulbed	/rdz/	cards
/kts/	acts	/rbd/	barbed	/ndz/	sands
/fts/	lifts	/lvd/	delved	/lmz/	films
/lθs/	tilths	/rvd/	carved	/rmz/	arms
/rθs/	hearths	/lmd/	filmed	/lnz/	kilns
/nθs/	months	/rmd/	armed	/rnz/	turns
/ŋθs/	lengths	/lnd/	kilned	/rlz/	curls
/dθs/	widths	/rnd/	turned	/lvz/	delves
/tθs/	eighths	/rld/	curled	/rvz/	carves
/lfs/	Alf's	/nzd/	bronzed	/rgz/	bergs
/ltšt/	filched	/mpts/	tempts	/ltst/	waltzed
/rtšt/	marched	/rtst/	quartzed	/rldz/	worlds
/ntšt/	pinched	/ŋkst/	minxed	/ŋkts/	instincts
/ldžd/	bulged	/mpst/	glimpsed	/lfθs/	twelfths
/rdžd/	charged	/rpts/	excerpts	/ntst/	chintzed
/ndžd/	changed	/ksθs/	sixths	/lkts/	mulcts
/ksts/	texts	/rsts/	thirsts		

V. Simplification of Consonant Clusters

Because the pronunciation of consonant clusters is relatively difficult even for native speakers of English, ways are found to simplify their pronunciation. Native speakers of English will often pronounce *find it* as /fayn-dɪt/ or *charged out* as /tšardž-dawt/, thus breaking a cluster between syllables and making it easier to say.

This process is called "phonetic syllabication."[2] It occurs most often when a final consonant cluster precedes a word beginning with a vowel sound. The final consonant of the cluster moves forward to the next syllable and is pronounced with the initial vowel of that syllable.

Sometimes a final cluster made up of three consonants is reduced by the omission of one of the consonants. This happens most often when the medial consonant is a voiceless stop sound: *acts* /ækts/ becomes /æks/, *lifts* /lɪfts/ becomes /lɪfs/, *asked* /æskt/ becomes /æst/. Another example of consonant cluster reduction is *depths* /dɛpθs/ which is often pronounced /dɛps/.

We do not wish to overemphasize the simplification of consonant clusters, but it seems useful to suggest that students whose native language does not permit such complex sequences as are found in English make use of consonant cluster reduction and phonetic syllabication to as great an extent as possible. However, there is no way that a student can avoid the necessity of pronouncing a great number of consonant clusters which are an essential part of the sound system of English.

VI. Exercises

A. 1. Pronounce the following words, paying particular attention to the initial consonant clusters.

a.	three	h.	through	o.	ground
b.	place	i.	program	p.	creature
c.	class	j.	green	q.	glance
d.	trouble	k.	free	r.	fly
e.	float	l.	pretty	s.	blanket
f.	practice	m.	drink	t.	floor
g.	great	n.	blade	u.	prize

2. This exercise is particularly helpful for those who have difficulty with initial consonant clusters with the /s/-sound. Pronounce each word, concentrating on the /s/-sound and lengthening it, if necessary, making sure you do not insert a vowel sound before it. Then pronounce the words at a more normal speed.

a.	sweater	d.	star	g.	schedule
b.	spiral	e.	spot	h.	special
c.	struggle	f.	snow	i.	slide

---

[2]This term is borrowed from Tomás Navarro Tomás. See T. Navarro Tomás and Aurelio M. Espinosa, *A Primer of Spanish Pronunciation* (New York, 1926).

j. smile	n. string	r. small
k. splash	o. splurge	s. sky
l. spray	p. sphere	t. sniffle
m. scratch	q. squint	u. scream

B. 1. Read the phrases below which contain final consonant clusters. Simplify them by using phonetic syllabication; that is, pronounce the final consonant of the cluster as if it were the initial consonant of the second word: *cooks it* /kʊks ɪt/ as /kʊk-sɪt/.

a. almost a year	k. caused it	
b. last a year	l. fills it	
c. just a year	m. returned it	
d. best of all	n. loves it	
e. most of all	o. works it	
f. understands it	p. helped it	
g. recommends it	q. arranged it	
h. finds it	r. thinks it	
i. loans it	s. changed it	
j. runs it	t. curled it	

2. Read the following phrases which *cannot* be simplified by phonetic syllabication. Be sure you pronounce all of the consonants.

a. don't know	k. that's clear	
b. last minute	l. most boys	
c. thank them	m. it's broken	
d. can't think	n. can't quite	
e. gets back	o. depth from	
f. doesn't rain	p. looked through	
g. think so	q. first quarter	
h. forward march	r. works perfectly	
i. six feet	s. sounds pretty	
j. first floor	t. just three	

C. Because the word *the* occurs so frequently in English, it seems useful to practice phrases with the word *the* preceded by words which contain final consonant clusters. You will notice that, with a little practice, your tongue adjusts itself to various points of articulation for /ð/, depending upon the consonant which precedes it. Practice reading these phrases several times until you can say them smoothly.

1. changed the room	3. aren't the ones
2. failed the test	4. assumed the worst

5. hopped the fence	13. sort the cards
6. helped the man	14. since the dance
7. worth the trouble	15. understand the word
8. built the house	16. almost the end
9. amazed the people	17. thinks the most
10. deals the cards	18. points the arrow
11. worked the puzzle	19. knows the date
12. fixed the machine	20. it's the end

D. 1. Read the sentences below, all of which have singular subjects. Pay particular attention to the pronunciation of the final consonant clusters in the verb forms: /-lts/ *consults*, /-ks/ *looks*. Then read the sentences again, making the subject of each sentence plural and paying attention to the final consonant clusters of the noun forms: /-rz/ *lawyers*, /-mz/ *rooms*.

   a. The lawyer consults many books.

   b. The room looks empty.

   c. The example seems easy.

   d. The instructor writes on the blackboard.

   e. The teacher smiles at the class.

   f. The student tells stories.

   g. The girl sings beautifully.

   h. The professor answers the questions.

   i. The girl receives letters every day.

   j. The picture hangs on the wall.

   2. Your teacher will read one of the sentences above, sometimes with a singular subject, sometimes with a plural subject. You will tell her which she is pronouncing. This will give you practice in listening for the -s ending. Individual students can continue the exercise.

E. 1. Read the sentences below, all of which have present verb forms. Then read the sentences changing the verbs to the past form. Pay attention to the final consonant clusters which are formed by the addition of the -ed ending.

   a. They live on Main Street.

   b. We study very hard.

   c. They ask a lot of questions.

      d.   The professor always answers them.

      e.   The janitors mop the floor.

      f.   The boys laugh a lot.

      g.   The waitress serves breakfast.

      h.   We arrange the date of the dance.

      i.   The twins look alike.

      j.   We prepare a list.

2.   Your teacher will read a sentence from above, sometimes in the present tense, sometimes in the past. You will tell her which she is pronouncing. This will give you practice in listening for the -ed ending. Individual students can continue the exercise.

F.   This drill is intended to give you practice in pronouncing difficult combinations of consonants without inserting a "finishing sound." Be particularly careful with the combinations which involve an initial **s** followed by a consonant, as you pronounce the entire exercise several times. Use phonetic syllabication to simplify consonant clusters where possible. This material is well suited to individual laboratory work.

    1.   A large group of students graduates each spring.

    2.   I heard that splendid speech you made last night.

    3.   He changed his mind and lunched at the student cafeteria.

    4.   They answered correctly, and the instructor thanked them.

    5.   I request that all books be removed from the desks.

    6.   He will need all his strength to catch the others.

    7.   The next time you come we must speak Swahili.

    8.   Someone's trying to turn my friends against me.

    9.   Does she like this part of the United States?

   10.   George nudged me and asked if we hadn't watched long enough.

   11.   I wonder why that child acts so strangely.

   12.   The baby has a big splinter in the skin of his finger.

   13.   Thanksgiving comes the last Thursday in November.

   14.   Do you expect to catch the next train?

   15.   We'll have to risk using the old screens this year.

G.   Read the following paragraph, paying particular attention to final consonant clusters produced by the -ed ending.

Clarence, a university student who lives with his aunt in town, often helps around the house. One Saturday, his aunt went downtown, leaving a list of things for Clarence to do. Clarence performed the first three chores with great good will. Then he discovered that his car had a flat tire. He changed it and began to work on the engine. When his aunt arrived home, she found that Clarence had washed the dishes, made his bed, and picked up his clothes. But he hadn't washed the windows, burned the trash, hosed down the front porch, or trimmed the hedge. Clarence confessed that the time had slipped by, and he was very sorry.

With your book closed, talk about all the things that Clarence had done and had not done.

H. Read the following paragraph paying particular attention to final consonant clusters produced by the -s̲ ending.

Clarence's brother George lives at home with their parents. George's life is different from that of Clarence, and Clarence sometimes envies him. George eats big breakfasts every day. He seldom reads a book and never writes letters. He often tinkers with his car or plays baseball in the afternoon. He makes dates with girls on the weekends, but otherwise he never keeps a schedule. He earns money at odd jobs and spends it freely. He takes life lightly. Clarence remembers that his own life used to be as carefree as this before he entered the university.

With your book closed, talk about all the things that George does in his carefree life.

I. Practice reading aloud articles from the newspaper, paying particular attention to the smooth pronunciation of consonant clusters.

Long and Short Vowels

I. The Theory of Long and Short Vowels

Lessons 10 and 11 were designed to help you avoid that type of vowel substitution which is due to inability to hear or reproduce clearly an English vowel which does not exist as a distinctive sound or is formed differently in your mother tongue. This lesson and the one following are aimed at the other types of difficulty students may have in giving the stressed vowel of a word its correct value: vowel substitutions caused by the inconsistencies of English spelling, or the differences between the English and some other system of spelling. In order to approach the problem, we must examine such relationships as may exist between vowel sounds and the way they are ordinarily spelled.

For many years a great many English grammars in various countries of the world have taught the theory of "long" and "short" vowels. This is also the theory behind the system of diacritical marks used in many of our dictionaries: a straight line is placed over long vowels, as in *lāte;* a curved line over short vowels, as in *păt.*

In its simplest form, the theory is that each of the five English vowels—a, e, i, o, u—has two most common sounds *in stressed syllables*, a long sound and a short sound.

LETTER	LONG SOUND		SHORT SOUND	
a	/ey/	lāte	/æ/	păt
e	/iy/	ēve	/ɛ/	ĕnd
i	/ay/	īce	/ɪ/	sĭt
o	/ow/	ōld	/a/	ŏdd
u	/yuw/	cūbe	/ə/	ŭp

You will notice that the long sounds of the vowels have been phonetically transcribed in this text as vowel plus glide. It is also worth mentioning that the name of the vowel letter is pronounced the same as the long sound which that letter represents; for example, the name of the letter a is pronounced /ey/, which is also the pronunciation of the long sound of that letter. Perhaps the short sounds of the vowel letters can be called nicknames of the letters; for example, /æ/ is the *nickname* of the letter a, while /ey/ is its *name*.

Each vowel is pronounced with its *long* sound

1.   If it is final in the syllable:

pā-per, shē, fī-nal, nō, dū-ty

2.   If it is followed by an unpronounced e, or a consonant plus an unpronounced e:

māke, ēve, dīe, Pōe, ūse

Each vowel is pronounced with its *short* sound,

1.   If it is followed in the same syllable by a consonant:

măt-ter, wĕnt, rĭv-er, dŏc-tor, cŭt

It should be remembered that these "rules" apply only to vowels in *stressed* syllables; we already know that, when *unstressed*, almost all vowels are pronounced /ə/ or /ɪ/.

Notice, too, that the difference between the long and short sounds of a given letter is not a matter of the length of time it takes to pronounce the vowel, but is a result of a difference in the position of the tongue. (These differences in tongue position were discussed in Lessons 10 and 11.)

II. Stressed Vowels Followed by a Consonant, Then by Another Vowel Sound

One limitation of the theory is that it does not explain clearly the pronunciation of the vowels in words like *ever* and *even*, where the stressed vowel is followed by a consonant and then by another vowel sound. Is the e of *ever* in a long or short position; is it final in the syllable or followed in the same syllable by a consonant? In other words, is the v a part of the first syllable or the second? If v is the last sound in the first syllable, then the e is in a short position and should be pronounced /ɛ/; if v is part of the second syllable, e is in a long position and should be pronounced as /iy/. But how can a student know where the syllables of the word are to be divided? If he looks up the rules for the division of syllables, he will find that a consonant between two vowel sounds, such as the v in *ever*, goes with the first syllable if the preceding vowel is short, and with the second syllable if the preceding vowel is long. This information, of course, leads him in a vicious circle and is useless unless the student already knows how to pronounce the e of *ever*. The theory of long and short vowels could not have helped him to determine the pronunciation of an unknown word of the type of *ever* and *even*. He must simply learn that *ever* is pronounced /ɛ́v-ər/, and *even* /íy-vən/.

Actually, the situation with regard to words of this kind—in which the stressed vowel is followed by a consonant and then another vowel sound—varies with each vowel.

THE LETTER i USUALLY HAS A SHORT SOUND.

SHORT /ɪ/: addition, British, citizen, city, civil, condition, consider, continue, division, familiar, figure, finish, given, image, individual, Italy, liberty, lily, limit, linen, magnificent, military, minister, minute, opinion, original, particular, Philip, physician, pity, position, prison, religious, spirit, sufficient, Virginia.

LONG /ay/: China, climate, final, Friday, private, silence, tiny.

THE LETTER e USUALLY HAS A SHORT SOUND.

SHORT /ɛ/: American, benefit, celebrate, credit, delicate, develop, devil, eleven, enemy, especial, ever, general, generous, level, medicine, memory, merit, necessary, never, perish, precious, présent, president, recognize, récord, register, regular, relative, second, senate, separate, seven, special, telephone.

LONG /iy/: convenient, Egypt, equal, even, evil, female, fever, frequent, immediate, Peter, recent, region.

THE LETTER o HAS LONG AND SHORT SOUNDS WITH ALMOST EQUAL FREQUENCY.

SHORT /a/: body, colony, column, copy, holiday, honest, honor, model, moderate, modern, modest, monument, olive, probable, product, profit, promise, proper, property, province, Robert, robin, solid, Thomas, volume.

LONG /ow/: broken, frozen, Joseph, local, locate, moment, motion, notice, ocean, October, open, over, pony, Roman, sober, total.

THE LETTER a HAS LONG AND SHORT SOUNDS WITH
ALMOST EQUAL FREQUENCY.

SHORT /æ/: animal, avenue, balance, chapel, companion, examine, family, gradual, habit, imagine, Italian, Latin, magic, manage, national, natural, palace, rapid, salary, satisfy, Saturday, shadow, Spanish, statue, travel, value, vanish, wagon.

LONG /ey/: Asia, baby, education, famous, favor, favorite, foundation, gracious, information, invitation, labor, lady, lazy, maker, naked, nation, native, nature, navy, paper, patience, patient, population, potato, relation, station, vapor.

THE LETTER u ALMOST ALWAYS HAS A LONG SOUND.

SHORT /ə/: punish, study.

LONG /yuw/: funeral, future, human, humor, music, numerous, opportunity, peculiar, pupil, uniform, union, usual.

The examples above include most of the common words of the type here considered. It would be well to check over the lists carefully and mark any items which you would have hesitated to pronounce. Almost all students are doubtful regarding certain words like these, in which the spelling gives no clear indication of the pronunciation.

If you need to pronounce unfamiliar words of this kind, you should consult a dictionary whenever possible. If you have to guess, however, you may do so with some degree of certainty when the stressed vowel is i, e, or u.[1] Thus you could be fairly sure that the i of *tibia* is to be given the sound of /ɪ/, and that the e of *senary* is /ɛ/. You could be practically certain that the u of *cuticle* is pronounced as /yuw/.

You may find the preceding explanation easier to remember if you will note that, in the type of word we have been discussing, the

---

[1]An examination of the 2,500 most common English words, as listed in E. L. Thorndike, *The Teacher's Word Book*, reveals that i is short in 79% of the pertinent cases, e in 75%, o in 64%, a in 55%, and u in only 20%. If we examine a larger number of words, thus including more bookish and unusual terms, the proportion of short vowels is: i, 70%; e, 76%; o, 63%; a, 45%; and u, 10%.

letters we associate with front vowels, i̱ and e̱, tend to have their short sound. The letter we associate with back vowels, u̱, usually has its long sound. The middle vowels, o̱ and a̱, may be long or short.

III. Limitations and Values of the Theory

Another limitation, and a very important one, of the theory of long and short vowels is that a very large number of common words are simply not pronounced according to the rules, and must therefore be thought of as exceptions. For example, the letter i̱ in the short position (followed in the same syllable by a consonant) should be pronounced /ɪ/, but in practice is pronounced /ay/ almost as frequently: *child* /tšayld/, *kind* /kaynd/, *light* /layt/. If the theory of long and short vowels is to be of value to you, you must keep in mind that its rules merely call attention to tendencies and are less perfect even than many other so-called laws of language. There is a large group of words the pronunciation of which could not be explained by any set of rules, however complicated, and which must therefore be learned individually.

A very large number of vowels are not pronounced according to the theory when they are followed by ḻ or ṟ. Because of the movements made by the speech organs in preparing to pronounce these two consonants (see Lesson 9, Sections I and II), ḻ and ṟ tend to make any vowel which precedes them have more of a back sound than it would normally have. Thus, a̱ in the short position is usually pronounced /æ/: *actor* /ǽktər/; but a̱ in the short position followed by ḻ is ordinarily pronounced /ɔ/: *alter* /ɔ́ltər/. And a̱ in the short position followed by ṟ usually has the sound of /a/: *arm* /a̱rm/.

TABLE SHOWING HOW VOWELS FOLLOWED BY Ḻ OR Ṟ VARY
FROM THE SOUND THEY SHOULD HAVE ACCORDING TO THE
THEORY OF LONG AND SHORT VOWELS

a̱

IN LONG POSITION

Normal sound, according to theory	/ey/, la̱te /leẙt/
Followed by ḻ	/eə/, sa̱le /seəl/
Followed by ṟ	/ɛə/, ca̱re /kɛər/

IN SHORT POSITION

Normal sound, according to theory	/æ/, sa̱t /sæt/
Followed by ḻ	/ɔ/, a̱lter /ɔ́ltər/
Followed by ṟ	/a/, ca̱r /ka̱r/

e   IN LONG POSITION

Normal sound, according to theory	/iy/, even /íyvən/
Followed by l	(rare)
Followed by r	/ɪə/, here /hɪər/

                                IN SHORT POSITION

Normal sound, according to theory	/ɛ/, met /mɛt/
Followed by l	/ɛə/, well /wɛəl/
Followed by r	/ə(ər)/, verb /vərb/

i   IN LONG POSITION

Normal sound, according to theory	/ay/, mine /mayn/
Followed by l	(same)
Followed by r	(same)

                                IN SHORT POSITION

Normal sound, according to theory	/ɪ/, hit /hɪt/
Followed by l	/ɪə/, hill /hɪəl/
Followed by r	/ə(ər)/, sir /sər/

o   IN LONG POSITION

Normal sound, according to theory	/ow/, rose /rowz/
Followed by l	(same)
Followed by r	(same)

                                IN SHORT POSITION

Normal sound, according to theory	/a/, hot /hat/
Followed by l	/ow/, cold /kowld/
Followed by r	/ɔ/, for /fɔr/

u No variation

      A third limitation of the theory of long and short vowels is that the terms it uses are not scientifically accurate, in the sense that more time is frequently taken in forming so-called "short" vowels than in forming "long" ones. The words "short" and "long" should mean that short vowels require less time to pronounce than long ones. Yet the long e of *beat* /biyt/ is a shorter sound than the short i of *bid* /bɪːd/. In the sentence "His name is John," the short o of *John* is surely longer than the long a of *name*. The vowel of *bid* is long because it is followed by a voiced consonant, and that of *beat* is short because it is followed by a voiceless consonant (see Lesson 8, Section II). In the particular sentence cited above, the o of *John* is unusually long because it must be pronounced on both the high and low tones of the intonation pattern (see Lesson 5, Section II).

In spite of its limitations, however, the theory of long and short vowels is the most successful attempt which has yet been made to explain, logically and with relative simplicity, the relationship between the spelling and the sounds of English vowels. In view of the large number of pronunciation errors which even advanced students of English make because of their lack of clear associations between vowel sounds and their usual spelling, it is worth your while to familiarize yourself with the theory, or renew your acquaintance with it. You will then be in a position to identify words of irregular pronunciation more easily, and to concentrate on learning them individually.

The theory should also be a help to you in the troublesome problem of dividing words by a hyphen at the end of a line of writing. Remember that long vowels usually end a syllable (except when followed by a consonant plus a silent e), but short vowels do not. If you happen to know how the first vowel in *finish* /fíniš/ and *final* /fáynl̩/ is pronounced, you can be sure that the n of *finish* goes with the first syllable, *fin-ish;* and that the n of *final* goes with the second, *fi-nal.*

IV. Exercises

A. 1. What English vowel sounds do not exist in your mother tongue?

2. In your mother tongue, is it possible to find two words of different meaning exactly alike in sound except that one contains an /iy/ and the other an /ɪ/ (such as *seat* /siyt/ and *sit* /sɪt/ in English)? Do /ey/ and /ɛ/ ever constitute the only difference between two words? /ɛ/ and /æ/? /æ/ and /a/? /ɔ/ and /ow/? /ə/ and /a/?

3. Which English vowels and diphthongs do you have most difficulty in pronouncing?

4. Do you sometimes make the mistake of pronouncing *up* as /ap/ instead of /əp/? Why? (See Lesson 10, Section I.) Do you ever confuse /ʊ/ and /ə/? Why? Did you ever mispronounce *post* as /past/ instead of /powst/; *wash* as /wæš/ instead of /waš/? If so, can you explain the reason for the mispronunciation?

B. 1. What are the long and short sounds of a̲, e̲, i̲, o̲, and u̲?

2. According to the theory, should the *stressed* vowel in the following words be long or short?

a.	age	i.	less	q.	doctor
b.	lake	j.	nine	r.	number
c.	expect	k.	box	s.	happen
d.	I	l.	just	t.	complete
e.	bone	m.	escape	u.	begin
f.	suppose	n.	cent	v.	which
g.	ask	o.	see	w.	go
h.	be	p.	tie	x.	use

Are all of the words in this list actually pronounced according to the theory?

3. Which of the following very common words have stressed vowels which are *not* pronounced according to the theory of long and short vowels as explained in this lesson?

a.	any	i.	hundred	q.	then
b.	busy	j.	other	r.	water
c.	have	k.	sing	s.	bottom
d.	only	l.	watch	t.	gone
e.	race	m.	both	u.	no
f.	was	n.	glass	v.	put
g.	blue	o.	move	w.	these
h.	give	p.	pure	x.	wrong

C. 1. The stressed vowel in each of the words below is followed by a consonant, then by another vowel sound. You will remember that the spelling gives very little help in pronouncing such combinations of letters (see Section II of this lesson). Can you give each stressed vowel its proper sound?

a.	ávenue	i.	línen	q.	récognize
b.	convénient	j.	nátural	r.	tótal
c.	hóliday	k.	récent	s.	cólony
d.	nátive	l.	tíny	t.	fínal
e.	púnish	m.	clímate	u.	náked
f.	róbin	n.	évil	v.	próvince
g.	cívil	o.	móment	w.	récord
h.	dévil	p.	númerous	x.	vápor

2. What would be the safest guess as to the vowel sound in the stressed syllable of each of these rather rare words?

a. fácet	e. múcous	i. sésame
b. mímic	f. ríbald	j. húmic
c. péncil	g. fócal	k. nícotine
d. fétus	h. nématode	l. tríad

Look up each word in a dictionary and see how often you guessed correctly.

D. Pronounce the following pairs of words several times, and notice how the presence of an l or r changes the sound of the vowel in each case (see Section III of this lesson).

1. cat, cart	10. mane, male	18. fist, first
2. had, hard	11. gem, germ	19. sick, silk
3. case, care	12. beg, berg	20. sit, silt
4. date, dare	13. ten, tern	21. spot, sport
5. bad, bald	14. mete, mere	22. stock, stork
6. sat, salt	15. met, melt	23. cod, cold
7. back, balk	16. sped, spelled	24. God, gold
8. after, alter	17. bid, bird	25. cot, colt
9. save, sale		

Write the phonetic symbol which represents the vowel of each word.

E. 1. Keeping in mind that long vowels usually end syllables and short vowels do not, divide these words into syllables.

a. bacon	f. motor	k. notion
b. metal	g. together	l. pupil
c. promise	h. punish	m. table
d. rival	i. second	n. mason
e. frozen	j. gather	o. pity

2. Why do you suppose the final p of *hop* is doubled when *-ing* is added? Why double the g of *big* when *-est* is added? Why double the b of *rob* when *-ed* is added?

F. Let the members of the class ask and answer questions about their school work. As they speak, the instructor should listen carefully and encourage them to diphthongize /ey/ and /ow/ slightly in cases where such diphthongization would be most natural: when the vowel is final, when it is followed by a final voiced consonant, or when it is pronounced with a glide at the end of an intonation pattern (see Lesson 10, Section IV). Key expressions for use in the questions might be: *grade, raise your grade, call the role, every day, an "A," know, fail, say, study load, closed section, go, at home, alone, show, loathe, what page, change sections, study aids.*

G. Work on the following passage[2] for naturalness of intonation and rhythm.

After you have prepared it carefully, this material may be recorded.

1. "Hello," he said.   2. She pushed her glasses up onto her forehead, as he kissed her.   3. "Listen, Marge, I don't want us to get our wires crossed.   4. I've made a date with Eddie to go fishing next Monday.

5. It's the opening of the season, so put that down in your book, will you?"   6. She looked at her engagement pad.   7. "Oh, Joe! But that's the night we dine with the Medfords, darling."   8. "Oh, oh!" he said,

"I knew there'd be a snag.   9. Have you accepted already?"

10. "Yes," she said, "of course."   11. "What do you mean 'of course'?" he said.   12. "Why on earth couldn't you have asked me about it, eh?

13. Then I'd have told you to keep the fifteenth clear."

---

[2]Adapted from the story "A Matter of Pride" by Christopher La Farge, originally published in the *New Yorker*.

H. Outside of class prepare several pages of a magazine article for reading aloud by marking the pauses by means of which it can best be divided into thought groups. Then read the article, being careful to blend your words together within thought groups. Try to avoid glottal stops and finishing sounds (see Lesson 4, Section IV).

Spelling and Vowel Sounds

I. The Relationship between Spelling and Sound

This lesson is an amplification of the fundamental material presented in Lesson 15. The most important relationships between the spelling and pronunciation of stressed vowels in English words are the result of the vowel's being in a "long" or "short" position, or of its being followed by an l or r. But it seems worth while to know also about certain other relationships of less general application: for example, the combination ea, which is normally pronounced /iy/ as in *each*, usually has the sound of /ɛ/ before a d—*bread, dead, head*.

Facts of this nature are included in the long table which follows. You are not expected to memorize the table. The exercises at the end of the lesson will help you to become familiar with it, and you may wish to refer to it later. It should be of help to you in your attempts to avoid that type of vowel substitution which is caused by the way in which a word is spelled.

Of course, it will never be possible to explain logically, by a neat set of rules, the spelling of *all* English vowel sounds. You will find that in some cases the exceptions are almost as numerous as the examples on which a "rule" is based. You should know of such relationships as do exist between sound and spelling, but you should also realize that even the clearest of these cannot always be trusted. In the final analysis, the pronunciation of many words must simply be learned individually. Pay particular attention to the exceptions listed below!

II. The Pronunciation of Stressed Vowels

VOWEL COMBINATION	PRO-NUNCI-ATION	EXAMPLES	COMMON EXCEPTIONS
1. a, in long position, normally	/ey/	face /feys/, brave /breyv/, shape /šeyp/, take /teyk/	have /hæv/ or /əv/; water /wɔtər/; father /faðər/
2. a, in long position, before l	/ee/	sale /seel/, male /meel/, pale /peel/, whale /hweel/	
3. a, in long position, before r	/εə/*	care /kεər/, square /skwεər/, dare /dεər/, rare /rεər/	are /ar/ or /ər/
4. a, in short position, normally	/æ/	ask /æsk/, man /mæn/, sad /sæd/, chance /tšæns/, bank /bæŋk/, last /læst/, pass /pæs/, bag /bæg/, path /pæθ/, sand /sænd/, fancy /fænsɪ/, master /mæstər/	able /eybəl/, table /teybəl/; change /tšeyndž/, strange /streyndž/; taste /teyst/, waste /weyst/; want /want/, watch /watš/, what /hwat/, wash /waš/, was /waz/ or /wez/; any /ɛnɪ/, many /mɛnɪ/
5. a, in short position, before l	/ɔ/	all /ɔl/, salt /sɔlt/, ball /bɔl/, talk /tɔk/	half /hæf/, shall /šæl/ or /šəl/
6. a, in short position, before r	/a/	art /art/, star /star/, car /kar/, charge /tšardž/	war /wɔr/, warm /wɔrm/, quarter /kwɔrtər/
7. ai, normally	/ey/	plain /pleyn/, raise /reyz/, wait /weyt/, paint /peynt/	again /əgɛn/, against /əgɛnst/, said /sɛd/
8. ai, before l	/ee/	sail /seel/, tail /teel/, mail /meel/, fail /feel/	

VOWEL COMBINATION	PRONUNCIATION	EXAMPLES	COMMON EXCEPTIONS
9. ai, before r	/ɛər/*	air /ɛər/, chair /tʃɛər/, hair /hɛər/, fair /fɛər/	
10. au	/ɔ/	cause /kɔz/, pause /pɔz/, Paul /pɔl/, daughter /dɔ́tər/	laugh /læf/
11. aw	/ɔ/	draw /drɔ/, law /lɔ/, saw /sɔ/, paw /pɔ/	
12. ay	/ey/	say /sey/, stay /stey/, ways /weyz/, day /dey/	says /sɛz/
13. e, in long position, normally	/iy/	be /biy/, he /hiy/, she /ʃiy/, these /ðiyz/, even /íyvən/	
14. e, in long position, before r	/ɪə/	here /hɪər/, mere /mɪər/, sphere /sfɪər/, sincere /sɪnsɪər/	there /ðɛər/, where /hwɛər/; were /wər/
15. e, in short position, normally	/ɛ/	best /bɛst/, dress /drɛs/, end /ɛnd/, fence /fɛns/	pretty /prɪti/
16. e, in short position, before l	/ɛə/	bell /bɛəl/, else /ɛəls/, help /hɛəlp/, twelve /twɛəlv/	
17. e, in short position,	/ə(ər)/	her /hər/, serve /sərv/, verb /vərb/, perfect /pə́rfɪkt/	
18. ea, normally	/iy/	each /iytʃ/, leave /liyv/, mean /miyn/, please /pliyz/, reach /riytʃ/, sea /siy/, speak /spiyk/, beast /biyst/, heat /hiyt/, stream /striym/, teach /tiytʃ/, weak /wiyk/	break /breyk/, great /greyt/; breakfast /brɛkfəst/, heaven /hɛ́vən/, heavy /hɛ́vɪ/ measure /mɛ́žər/, pleasant /plɛ́zənt/, pleasure /plɛ́žər/, death /dɛθ/ weather /wɛ́ðər/

VOWEL COMBINATION	PRO-NUNCI-ATION	EXAMPLES	COMMON EXCEPTIONS
19. ea, before d	/ɛ/	bread /brɛd/, dead /dɛd/, head /hɛd/, ready /ˈrɛdɪ/	bead /biyd/, lead (verb) /liyd/ read (present tense) /riyd/
20. ea, before l	/ie/	deal /diəl/, heal /hiəl/, real /riəl/, steal /stiəl/	health /hɛəlθ/
21. ea, before r, normally	/ɪe/	clear /klɪər/, dear /dɪər/, ear /ɪər/, hear /hɪər/	bear /bɛər/, tear (rip) /tɛər/, wear /wɛər/
22. ea, before r, and another consonant	/ə(ər)/	early /ˈərlɪ/, earth /ərθ/, learn /lərn/, heard /hərd/	heart /hart/
23. ee, normally	/iy/	deep /diyp/, feet /fiyt/, free /friy/, green /griyn/	been /bɪn/
24. ee, before l	/ie/	feel /fiəl/, wheel /hwiəl/, heel /hiəl/, steel /stiəl/	
25. ee, before r	/ɪe/	beer /bɪər/, cheer /tšɪər/, deer /dɪər/, queer /kwɪər/	
26. ei, normally	/iy/	either /ˈiyðər/, receive /rɪsiyv/, seize /siyz/	veil /vɛəl/; their /ðɛər/
27. ei, before g or n	/ey/	eight /eyt/, neighbor /ˈneybər/, weigh /wey/, reign /reyn/; rein /reyn/, vein /veyn/	height /hayt/
28. ew	/yuw/	few /fyuw/	grew /gruw/
29. ey	/ey/	they /ðey/, convey /kənˈvey/	eye /ay/
30. i; in long position	/ay/	die /day/, lie /lay/, drive /drayv/, arrive /əˈrayv/	give /gɪv/, live (verb) /lɪv/; iron /ˈayərn/

VOWEL COMBINATION	PRO-NUNCIATION	EXAMPLES	COMMON EXCEPTIONS
31. i, in short position, normally	/ɪ/	big /bɪg/, sing /sɪŋ/, fish /fɪš/, since /sɪns/	sign /sayn/, island /áyland/
32. i, in short position, before gh, ld, (final), or nd (final)	/ay/	high /hay/, night /nayt/; child /tšayld/, wild /wayld/; wind (verb) /waynd/, find /faynd/, mind /maynd/	wind (noun) /wɪnd/
33. i, in short position, before l	/ɪɛ/	ill /ɪɛl/, will /wɪɛl/, milk /mɪɛlk/, until /entɪɛl/	
34. i, in short position, before r	/ə(ər)/	bird /bərd/, first /fərst/, girl /gərl/, sir /sər/	
35. ie, normally	/iy/	chief /tšiyf/, piece /piys/, believe /bɪliyv/, grief /griyf/	friend /frɛnd/; also see i in long position.
36. ie, before l	/iə/	field /fiəld/, yield /yiəld/	
37. ie, before r	/ɪə/	pier /pɪər/, fierce /fɪərs/	
38. o, in long position	/ow/	go /gow/, no /now/, so /sow/, ago /əgów/; alone /əlówn/, close (verb) /klowz/, home /howm/, hope /howp/, stone /stown/, those /ðowz/, whole /howl/, bone /bown/, nose /nowz/, note /nowt/, smoke /smowk/, spoke /spowk/, suppose /sepówz/	do /duw/, into /íntuw/; to /tuw/ or /tə/, two /tuw/, who /huw/; move /muwv/, lose /luwz/, prove /pruwv/, whose /huwz/; gone /gɔn/; does /dəz/; shoe /šuw/; above /əbəv/, come /kəm/, done /dən/, love /ləv/, some /səm/, none /nən/; one /wən/

VOWEL COMBINATION	PRO-NUNCI-ATION	EXAMPLES	COMMON EXCEPTIONS
39. o̱, in short position, before a stop	/a/	box /baks/, drop /drap/, God /gad/, got /gat/, rock /rak/,	
40. o, in short position, before a contin-uant, normally	/ɔ/	across /əkrɔ́s/, along /əlɔ́ŋ/, corn /kɔrn/, cross /krɔs/, for /fɔr/, form /fɔrm/, long /lɔŋ/, lost /lɔst/, north /nɔrθ/, off /ɔf/, short /šɔrt/, soft /sɔft/, strong /strɔŋ/, born /bɔrn/, belong /bilɔ́ŋ/, cloth /klɔθ/, cost /kɔst/, lord /lɔrd/, loss /lɔs/, song /sɔŋ/, sort /sɔrt/, storm /stɔrm/, wrong /rɔŋ/, forth /fɔrθ/, report /rɪpɔ́rt/, morning /mɔ́rnɪŋ/, often /ɔ́fen/, order /ɔ́rdər/, corner /kɔ́rnər/, former /fɔ́rmər/, offer /ɔ́fər/, office /ɔ́fɪs/	woman /wúmen/; women /wímɪn/; whom /huwm/; once /wəns/; common /kámen/, follow /fálé/, possible /pásəbəl/; word /wərd/, work /wərk/, world /wərld/, worth /wərθ/; almost /ɔ́lmowst/, both /bowθ/, most /mowst/, don't /downt/, post /powst/, only /ównlɪ/; company /kə́mpenɪ/, wonder /wə́ndər/, tongue /təŋ/, among /əmə́ŋ/, front /frənt/, month /mənθ/, son /sen/, another /enə́ðər/, brother /brə́ðər/, color /kə́lər/, cover /kə́vər/, money /mə́nɪ/, mother /mə́ðər/, nothing /nə́θɪŋ/, other /ə́ðər/, discover /dɪskə́vər/, govern /gə́vern/

VOWEL COMBINATION	PRO-NUNCI-ATION	EXAMPLES	COMMON EXCEPTIONS
41. o, in short position, before l	/ow/	cold /kowld/, roll /rowl/, told /towld/, soldier /sówldžɑr/	
42. oa	/ow/	boat /bowt/, coal /kowl/, coast /kowst/	broad /brɔd/
43. oi	/ɔy/	point /pɔynt/, voice /vɔys/, noise /nɔyz/, soil /sɔyl/	
44. oo, final	/uw/	too /tuw/, woo /wuw/	
45. oo, before a stop	/ʊ/	hood /hʊd/, stood /stʊd/, good /gʊd/, wood /wʊd/, book /bʊk/, brook /brʊk/, cook /kʊk/, hook /hʊk/, look /lʊk/, shook /šʊk/, took /tʊk/, foot /fʊt/, soot /sʊt/	blood /blʌd/, flood /flʌd/; food /fuwd/, mood /muwd/, droop /druwp/, loop /luwp/, stoop /stuwp/, troop /truwp/, boot /buwt/, root /ruwt/, shoot /šuwt/
46. oo, before a continuant, normally	/uw/	room /ruwm/, school /skuwl/, soon /suwn/, moon /muwn/	
47. oo, before r	/ow/	door /dowr/, floor /flowr/	poor /pur/
48. ou, normally	/aw/	about /əbáwt/, around /əráwnd/, found /fawnd/, house /haws/, out /awt/, sound /sawnd/, south /sawθ/, cloud /klawd/, count /kawnt/, doubt /dawt/, loud /lawd/, mouth /mawθ/	brought /brɔt/, thought /θɔt/, though /ðow/, although /ɔlðow/; through /θruw/, you /yuw/; country /kə́ntrɪ/ double /də́bəl/, enough /ɪnə́f/, touch /tətš/, trouble /trə́bəl/, young /yəŋ/

VOWEL COMBINATION	PRONUNCIATION	EXAMPLES	COMMON EXCEPTIONS
49. ou, before l or r, normally	/ow/	soul /sowl/, shoulder /šówlder/; course /kowrs/, four /fowr/, court /kowrt/, pour /powr/	your /yur/; journey /džérnı/; our /awr/, hour /awr/
50. ou, before final ld	/u/	could /kud/, should /šud/, would /wud/	
51. ow	/ow/ or /aw/	bow (weapon, or knot) /bow/, blow /blow/, flow /flow/, grow /grow/, know /now/, low /low/, own /own/, row (line, or to propel with oars) /row/, show /šow/, slow /slow/, snow /snow/, throw /Θrow/, toward /towrd/; bow (point of boat, or to incline) /baw/, allow /eláw/, down /dawn/, brown /brawn/, how /haw/, now /naw/, cow /kaw/, row (disturbance) /raw/, crowd /krawd/, town /tawn/, crown /krawn/, flower /flawr/	
52. oy	/ɔy/	boy /bɔy/, destroy /dıstrɔ́y/, joy /džɔy/, toy /tɔy/	
53. u, in long position	/yuw/	use /yuwz/, pure /pyuwr/, music /myúwzık/	rule /ruwl/, blue /bluw/
54. u, in short position	/e/ or /er/	but /bet/, rush /reš/, run /ren/, jump /džemp/, dull /del/, burn /bern/, hurt /hert/, us /se/	busy /bízı/; truth /truwΘ/; full /ful/, pull /pul/, put /put/, sugar /šúger/
Other common words in which u has an unusual sound: guard /gard/; build /bıld/; buy /bay/; fruit /fruwt/, suit /suwt/.			
55. y	/ay/	by /bay/, fly /flay/, cry /kray/, sky /skay/, supply /seplay/	

III. Exercises

A. 1. As you come across new words in your reading, add examples of your own to illustrate the vowel combinations in the preceding table.

2. Each of the following words is an example of one of the combinations in the table. Give the number of the combination illustrated by each word.

a.	set	o.	proud	cc.	dread
b.	fare	p.	boss	dd.	not
c.	seal	q.	rain	ee.	piece
d.	peel	r.	deceive	ff.	call
e.	third	s.	may	gg.	melt
f.	stew	t.	caught	hh.	hat
g.	search	u.	verse	ii.	freight
h.	meet	v.	oats	jj.	pair
i.	five	w.	fold	kk.	such
j.	hid	x.	lawn	ll.	cute
k.	cool	y.	name	mm.	crook
l.	shield	z.	farm	nn.	moth
m.	cede	aa.	ale	oo.	straight
n.	toil	bb.	blind	pp.	sigh

B. You may not be familiar with most of the following words, but all are pronounced regularly according to the rules formulated in this lesson. How should each be pronounced? Remember that the rules cited in the table refer only to *stressed* vowels. You already know (Lesson 3) the sounds usually given to unstressed vowels.

1.	ábbacy	15.	paunch	29.	mércurate
2.	taut	16.	pert	30.	streak
3.	abstérge	17.	tread	31.	weald
4.	delve	18.	hearse	32.	deign
5.	yearn	19.	veer	33.	wince
6.	drear	20.	abéyance	34.	besmírch
7.	askéw	21.	rind	35.	fiend
8.	hind	22.	frieze	36.	cajóle
9.	filch	23.	stooge	37.	bólster
10.	tier	24.	wold	38.	pounce
11.	thong	25.	slouch	39.	smalt
12.	bourn	26.	rebúke	40.	subvéne
13.	spume	27.	scald	41.	sere
14.	sparse	28.	abéle	42.	earl

43.	blear	46.	dirge	49.	rook
44.	skein	47.	wield	50.	bulge
45.	tithe	48.	loft	51.	vizíer

C. The words in the list below are all exceptions to our list of rules. Be sure you know exactly what sound should be given to the stressed vowel in each of them; look them up in the dictionary if necessary. Then identify the rule to which each is an exception.

1.	pear	8.	foul	15.	tough
2.	realm	9.	youth	16.	scoop
3.	machíne	10.	glove	17.	Tom
4.	plead	11.	doll	18.	beard
5.	bull	12.	swamp	19.	deaf
6.	calm	13.	awárd	20.	key
7.	ninth	14.	aunt	21.	cough

D. Write the phonetic symbol which represents the vowel sound in each of the words below which is an exception to the rules. Then read the entire list several times.

1.	do	17.	go	33.	move	49.	stove
2.	above	18.	prove	34.	love	50.	wove
3.	lose	19.	those	35.	whose	51.	nose
4.	none	20.	gone	36.	stone	52.	bone
5.	done	21.	does	37.	shoes	53.	foes
6.	both	22.	cloth	38.	come	54.	home
7.	some	23.	dome	39.	word	55.	lord
8.	worth	24.	north	40.	most	56.	cost
9.	post	25.	lost	41.	wonder	57.	ponder
10.	among	26.	long	42.	son	58.	on
11.	mother	27.	bother	43.	other	59.	cover
12.	over	28.	govern	44.	clover	60.	blood
13.	good	29.	food	45.	wood	61.	flood
14.	boot	30.	foot	46.	root	62.	soot
15.	blow	31.	how	47.	flow	63.	cow
16.	grown	32.	town	48.	crown	64.	own

E. The sentences in each of the following groups have the same rhythm and intonation. Sentence stresses are marked. Repeat each group until you can produce that particular pattern rapidly and smoothly. (This material is suitable for recording.)

1. a. To téll us to be quíet is unréasonable.

    b. The ówner is prepáred to redécorate it.

    c. I'll hélp you with your cóat when you're réady for it.

    d. I thínk he would be shócked if you ásked him for it.

    e. I néver would have thóught you would gíve it to me.

2. a. Have you stúdied your léssons?

    b. Does he spéak with an áccent?

    c. Is it wróng to get ángry?

    d. Are you wílling to téll me?

    e. Can you éver belíeve it?

3. a. I have exáms in mathemátics and chémistry.

    b. I would have thóught it was a Líncoln or a Cádillac.

    c. Was he idéntified befórehand or áfterward?

    d. You'll have to prómise me to lóve it and chérish it.

    e. Do you preférr to have it tóasted or úntoasted?

4. a. With a néw cár and enóugh tíme we could máke it.

    b. It's a lóng tíme since he léft hóme for the cíty.

    c. If you wón't gó, you can wríte nów and expláin it.

    d. When the wár énds and péace cómes, we'll be háppy.

    e. There's a fíne cúrrent of cóol áir near the wíndow.

F. The intonation patterns as marked in the sentences below are *not natural*. In fact, each sentence represents a type of "intonation error" often made by students. What suggestions could you make to help a person who used such patterns improve his speech?

1. How are you, Mr. Williams?

2. It's a beautiful day, isn't it?

3. What do you want with a dictionary?

4. How are you feeling this morning?

5. I think it's better over there, John.

6. Mr. Thomas is here, but I don't see Mrs. Thomas.

7. Is it a boy or a girl?

8. It's the center of our thoughts, our hopes, and our fears.

G. Outside of class practice reading several pages of a short story, concentrating your attention on a different feature at each reading: (1) intonation; (2) the correct formation of /r/; (3) syllabic consonants; (4) the correct pronunciation of the -s and -ed endings; (5) the smooth pronunciation of consonant clusters. In a final reading, try to combine all of these features satisfactorily.